NUCLEAR ACCIDENTS

BY JOEL HELGERSON

FRANKLIN WATTS I AN IMPACT BOOK
NEW YORK I LONDON I TORONTO I SYDNEY I 1988

FRONTIS (PAGE 6): AN ANTINUCLEAR-ENERGY DEMON-
STRATION IN PARIS AFTER THE CHERNOBYL ACCIDENT

Photographs courtesy of: Sygma: pp. 6 (Bernard Bisson), 49 (Jean-Louis
Atlan), 56, 67 top (Robert Gale), 73 top (Regis Bossu), 73 bottom (Julio
Donoso), 103 (Bill Pierce), 113 (Alain Nogues); Photo Researchers, Inc.:
pp. 10 (Bernard Pierre Wolff), 29 bottom (Omikron Collection), 31 both
(Paolo Koch), 33 and 38 (Kenneth Murray), 35 (Bonnie Freer), 97 (Michael
D. Sullivan), 99 top (Joseph S. Rychetnik), 99 bottom (Pavlovsky-Rapho);
Bettmann Archive, Inc.: pp. 21, 24; Tass from Sovfoto: pp. 29 top, 60, 67
bottom; UPI/Bettman Newsphotos: pp. 41, 53; AP/Wide World: pp. 86, 93.

Maps and diagrams by Vantage Art, Inc.

Library of Congress Cataloging-in-Publication Data

Helgerson, Joel.
Nuclear accidents.

(An Impact book)
Bibliography: p.
Includes index.
Summary: Describes nuclear fission and how nuclear reactors work and
discusses accidents at Chernobyl, Three Mile Island, and other power plants.
Also examines measures taken to prevent similar disasters in the future.
1. Nuclear power plants—Accidents—Juvenile literature. 2. Nuclear
reactors—Accidents—Juvenile Literature. (1. Nuclear power plants—
Accidents. 2. Nuclear reactors—Accidents) I. Title.
TK1078.H45   1988   363.1'79   87-21660
ISBN 0-531-10330-7

CONTENTS

NUCLEAR ACCIDENTS

THE REALITIES OF
NUCLEAR POWER

For over thirty years nuclear power has been a reality, yet many people around the world still do not trust its safety. They are uneasy about the potential dangers involved. Many people continue to oppose the use of nuclear reactors to generate electrical power. Protest groups have marched, demonstrated, and signed petitions in the United States, Britain, West Germany, Sweden, Italy, Hungary, and Japan. They voice concerns about their own safety and the safety of future generations.

What is unique about the dangers of nuclear power? Why do people protest its use?

The enormous destruction that can be released from the nucleus of atoms was first disclosed to the world when the United States dropped atomic bombs on the Japanese cities of Hiroshima and Nagasaki to end World War II. Since that time, many people have feared that nuclear energy could be used as a weapon of war. But it is impossible for a nuclear power plant to explode with the force of an atomic bomb. (This doesn't mean that a chemical explosion, such as from hydrogen igniting, can't happen in a nuclear power plant.) The greatest danger associated with nuclear power comes from one of its byproducts—radiation.

What is radiation? A form of it that we're all familiar with is light rays, which come in a wide range of frequencies, or wavelengths. Red light has the lowest frequency of all visible light; any radiation with a lower frequency can be felt as heat but can't be seen. Violet light has the highest frequency of light that is visible.

When applied to atomic science, radiation refers to the emission of three specific things: alpha particles, beta particles, and gamma rays. Alpha and beta particles (also often referred to as rays) contain high levels of energy. Gamma rays are similar to light or radio waves, but they differ in that they travel at much higher frequencies and consequently contain much more energy. It is the high energy level of these rays that creates problems for living organisms, by disrupting their cell structure. Strong doses of radiation can cause immediate death. Weaker doses can result in leukemia or other forms of cancer later in life.

In the course of our everyday life, radiation touches us all. When the dentist X-rays your teeth, extremely low levels of radiation are being used to help determine if you have cavities. The earth itself gives off a weak background radiation because of naturally occurring uranium and thorium, two elements that emit radiation. Radiation from outer space, in the form of cosmic rays, also daily bombards the earth. However, for the most part, our atmosphere shields us from these rays.

How can we know when the radiation around us has reached dangerous levels? We can't see radiation, or smell or touch it. And, as shown by the Soviet nuclear reactor accident of 1986 at Chernobyl, winds and rains can carry radioactive particles for hundreds, even thousands, of miles.

Another problem is the long-lasting nature of radiation. The release of radioactive energy can stretch across time—decades, even centuries—and continue to be dangerous.

So, nuclear power plants clearly do have the potential to kill, and an accident at a nuclear reactor could unleash this potential. But how likely is it that catastrophic accidents will occur? Or, perhaps an even more difficult question to answer: What constitutes a serious accident?

The amount of radiation released by an accident might serve as a good measure of the severity of that accident, but unfortunately scientists disagree over exactly how much radiation threatens life. It is not so much a question of what level of radiation causes *immediate* death as what level of radiation results in *total* deaths, including those that occur at a later date. Determining this presents real difficulties, because when death occurs years after exposure to the radiation, many other health factors can intervene.

Beyond the debate over the dangers of nuclear power, we need to consider another topic: What are the alternatives to nuclear power? And do these alternatives also present dangers?

As our population has grown, the supply of the earth's natural resources, including fossil fuels, has dwindled. And the use of certain fossil fuels (i.e., oil and coal) causes problems of pollution. This pollution takes its toll in human life, causing respiratory illness and cancer, ailments also associated with the release of radiation from nuclear reactor accidents.

Neither fossil fuels nor nuclear power offers complete safety, but some people believe that nuclear power is the best approach to solving at least our short-term energy needs. At present there are 375 nuclear power stations around the world that supply about 15 percent of the world's electricity. The United States has 93 nuclear power plants generating electricity.[1] The electricity that you use in your home or school for heat and light may be generated by nuclear reactors. Nuclear-generated electricity could be transformed into the energy needed to plow fields and feed people. Some countries already obtain over 50 percent of their electrical needs from atomic power.[2]

*The burning of oil (in the form of gasoline)
also causes pollution that kills.*

Nuclear energy can clearly help us meet our energy needs. But do its benefits outweigh its liabilities? The people who believe in the use of nuclear energy say yes. They either believe that it is already safe or that it can be made safe.

It would be preferable, say some who oppose nuclear power, to return to a complete dependence on fossil fuels. But we already know two things about these fuels. One, their pollution causes serious health problems. Two, they are a limited resource. At our present rate of consumption, fossil fuels such as oil would last for perhaps eighty years; known reserves of coal, on the other hand, could last another five hundred years.[3]

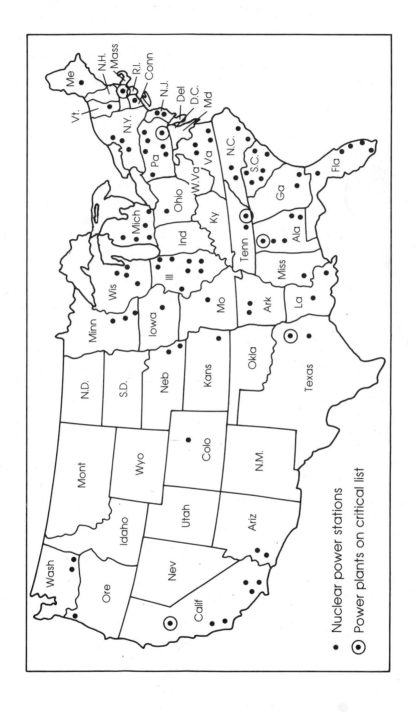

- Nuclear power stations
- ⊙ Power plants on critical list

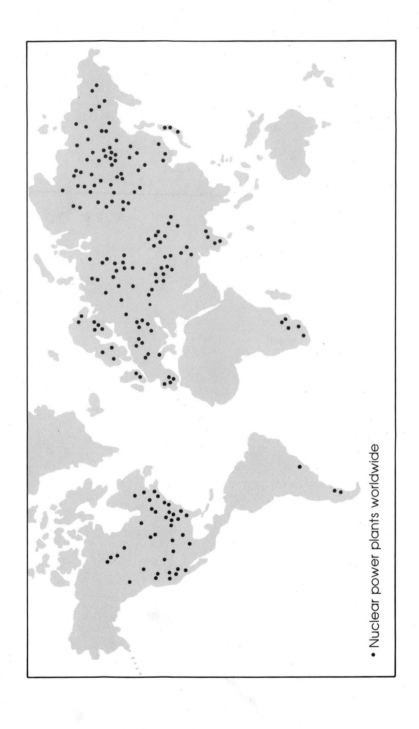

• Nuclear power plants worldwide

Some people believe that we could replace nuclear power with a combination of fossil fuels and other energy sources currently being developed, sources such as solar, wind, or geothermal energy. But will these alternative sources provide enough power inexpensively enough for our needs? Do they present their own safety problems? And can the burning of fossil fuels be safely managed?·

Two opposing camps of public opinion have evolved over the issue of nuclear power. The differences between these two groups are most visible when examining the problem of nuclear reactor accidents.

THE WORLD LEARNS
OF CHERNOBYL

On Monday morning at 9:00 A.M., April 28, 1986, western Europe began to detect the first evidence of the worst nuclear reactor accident in history. A technician at Sweden's Forsmark Nuclear Power Plant set off a radiation alarm by walking past it. After a quick examination, plant workers discovered that the blue covers protecting the technician's shoes contained enough radiation to set off the alarm.

The Forsmark Nuclear Power Plant sits 60 miles (96 km) north of Stockholm, Sweden's capital and a metropolitan area of over one million people. A nuclear accident so close to a major center would certainly have disastrous results.

The technicians at Forsmark first assumed that their own nuclear reactor was leaking. An evacuation of the plant was ordered and a hurried search for leaks began. Using a Geiger counter to test some of the plant's six hundred workers, it was discovered that a number of them were giving off radiation readings above the contamination levels allowable by plant standards. The radiation was being emitted from the workers' clothing. But inspection of the reactor soon indicated that the Forsmark plant wasn't the source of the radiation.

The technicians were seriously troubled. They had discovered a radiation leak whose source they couldn't pinpoint. The levels of radiation weren't yet lethal, but the technicians were concerned that they would increase before the source could be located. They began to take sample readings of the ground and plantlife near the reactor. These readings indicated radioactive emissions four to five times greater than normal.

Then other locations in Sweden began recording an increase in radioactivity; some readings jumped to over a hundred times the normal levels. This was bothersome, but still not high enough to immediately threaten life. Now the Swedes began to look outside their own country for the source of the radiation. They also released their findings to the rest of the world.

Some experts speculated that the residue of an underground nuclear test might have escaped into the atmosphere. But by 2:00 P.M. of that day, Swedish scientists had isolated radioactive isotopes of krypton, iodine, xenon, cesium, and cobalt—possible byproducts of a serious reactor core fire. (A later chapter discusses radioactive isotopes.) From this they deduced that the radioactivity must have originated in a nuclear reactor accident. Somewhere a nuclear reactor had suffered at least a partial meltdown of its core.[4]

As the day advanced, reports began to filter in from Finland to the north, Norway to the west, and Denmark to the south. Each country had recorded a leap in radiation levels. Scientists, studying weather patterns to determine where the radioactive materials might have come from, discovered that the wind during the preceding days had been coming from the southeast, from over the Black Sea. In its travel the wind whipped over the Russian republic of the Ukraine and then into White Russia and over the cool Baltic Sea. At an altitude of 5,000 feet (1,500 m) a stream of air rushed the radioactive cloud a thousand miles, first to the northeastern corner of Poland and southern Lithuania, then west to Finland and Sweden. The cloud didn't meet rain until it got to the Scandinavian mainland. Sweden was hit the hardest of all non-Eastern bloc countries, as winds blew steadily toward Scandinavia when the release of radioactive substances

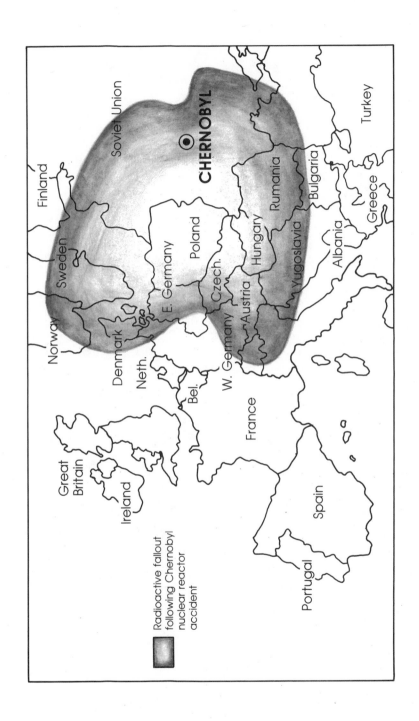

Radioactive fallout following Chernobyl nuclear reactor accident

was at its highest. Though radiation levels along the Swedish Baltic coast were five times normal, they were much higher in interior Sweden, north of Stockholm.[5]

It appeared that the accident must have occurred inside the Soviet Union. But when? And exactly where?

Using prevailing wind charts, meteorologists continued their analysis, and by late Monday they concluded that an accident had probably occurred at the Soviet Union's Chernobyl nuclear power plant. But the Chernobyl reactors were located 70 miles (113 km) north of Kiev, the Soviet Union's third largest city, with a population of two and a half million, and no news of an evacuation had come out of Kiev.

By this time the Swedish ambassador to the Soviet Union and other Swedish diplomats in Moscow had asked for an explanation from both the agency in charge of nuclear energy in the Soviet Union, the Soviet State Committee for the Use of Atomic Energy, and the Soviet government. But no answer was forthcoming. The Swedes were even reassured that if there had been a nuclear reactor accident, the Soviets would have notified Sweden of it!

Finally, at 9:00 P.M. that evening, a Russian television news program made the following brief announcement:

> An accident has occurred at the Chernobyl Nuclear Power Plant as one of the reactors was damaged. Measures are being taken to eliminate the consequences of the accident. Aid is being given to those affected. A government commission has been set up.[6]

With this announcement, the world knew for certain that an accident had happened, and because the released radiation had traveled as far as Sweden, it was obvious that a major accident had occurred.

But the news announcement left more questions unanswered than answered. How did the accident occur? When? What happened to the people in the vicinity? And why was the Soviet Union withholding information from the rest of the world?

Over the next weeks experts struggled to piece together an overall picture of the accident from the scant information released by the Soviets. Without doubt, the Chernobyl accident was the worst in the thirty-year history of the nuclear power industry. The questions raised by the accident may result in the improvement of nuclear reactor safety or, because of fear of similar or worse accidents, may bring about the closing of nuclear reactors in some parts of the world.

The remainder of this book examines the Chernobyl accident and other nuclear reactor accidents, discusses the consequences of such accidents, and attempts to provide some basic facts concerning the safety of nuclear power. The question of whether or not to continue using nuclear power will affect all of us and the generations that follow us. The nuclear power debate presents one of the most important questions facing people today, for without the great amounts of electricity created by nuclear energy, life for many people will change. But if we continue using nuclear power, life may also change. For better or for worse? Many people disagree on the answer to this.

2

NUCLEAR PHYSICS

Before examining nuclear accidents in more detail, we must take a look at how nuclear reactors operate. To help you understand all that you need to know, this chapter will briefly examine the scientific principles behind nuclear physics. The next chapter will discuss how those principles apply to nuclear reactors.

THE DISCOVERY OF RADIATION
By the 1800s scientists had determined that all matter was made up of atoms and that some matter could not be broken down into other substances by any means at their disposal. They called such substances *elements.* But beyond this, they had a great many questions about the structure of matter. For instance, they didn't know how to classify electricity. It didn't appear to be matter, so did this mean that it was made up of something other than atoms?

The scientific work that led to the principles behind nuclear reactors started with the investigation of what electricity is. As most often happens with important scientific discoveries, no one person was responsible. Rather, scientists built on each other's work. The first discovery of importance came after the invention of the vacuum tube. By sending electrical currents through a vacuum tube, scientists discovered that electricity crossed the tube in straight lines. They used the word *radiation* to label this phenomenon because the electricity traveled in a straight line just as rays of light radiated by the sun do.

Then, in 1897, an English scientist, Joseph Thomson (1856–1940), discovered that the particles that made up electricity's radiation were much smaller than atoms. Thomson called these subatomic particles *electrons* because they were found in electricity.

At about the same time a German scientist named Wilhelm Roentgen (1845–1923) discovered that when certain kinds of matter were bombarded by high-speed electrons, a different type of radiation was formed. Because he didn't know what kind of rays made up this radiation, he labeled them *X rays* (the "X" standing for unknown).

Hearing of Roentgen's discovery, a French scientist named Antoine Becquerel (1852–1908) showed that some compounds emitted X rays without being struck by electricity. Marie Curie (1867–1934), a Polish scientist, carried Becquerel's experiments a step further and showed that the element uranium—a part of the compound that Becquerel studied—emitted the radiation. She coined a new term by calling uranium *radioactive.*

THE SECRET OF THE ATOM
The discovery of radiation played a key role in helping to unlock the secrets of the structure of atoms. Once it was known that some types of matter (uranium, for example) radiated electrons, scientists realized that perhaps electricity was made up of the same things as ordinary matter after all. This led to further experiments showing that ultraviolet light, which has a high energy level, could push electrons out of some types of metal, leading to the conclusion that the electrons must be coming directly from

the atoms that made up the metal. Scientists now realized that atoms were made up of smaller particles, called *subatomic* particles.

When scientists investigated radiation, they discovered that it was made up of three types of rays—alpha, beta, and gamma rays (named after the first three letters of the Greek alphabet). By studying the effect of a magnet on these rays, scientists learned that the alpha and beta rays were made up of electrically charged particles. Because the alpha and beta particles curved in opposite directions when bent by a magnet, the alpha particle was considered to have a positive charge and the beta particle was considered to have a negative charge. The third type of ray—the gamma ray—was not affected by the magnet, and it was determined that gamma rays resembled light rays.

The next important discovery happened in 1914 when a New Zealand scientist named Ernest Rutherford (1871–1937) proved that subatomic particles could be combined to form elements. Rutherford carried out experiments in which trapped alpha particles were transformed into the element helium. The mass of the alpha particles and the mass of the helium atom produced were the same, so Rutherford reasoned that the alpha particles had combined with electrons, which have an extremely small mass, to form an atom of helium. By further experimenting, he proved that the helium atom was composed of an extremely small nucleus of a positive charge and a cloud of negatively charged electrons that surrounded the nucleus. The structure of the atom was becoming clearer.

The simplest element, hydrogen, has a single particle with a positive charge in its nucleus and a single electron of negative charge circling it. Rutherford labeled the single positive charge of the hydrogen nucleus a *proton.* Each of the 105 elements known to us today has a different number of protons in its nucleus and an equal number of electrons around it to balance the charge. Helium has 2 protons and 2 electrons; carbon has 6 protons, 6 electrons; oxygen: 8 protons, 8 electrons; iron: 26 pro-

Antoine Henri Becquerel   Ernest Rutherford

Marie Curie in her laboratory around 1905

tons, 26 electrons; uranium: 92 protons, 92 electrons. The number of protons in an element's nucleus is called its *atomic number.*

The picture of how elements were formed was becoming clearer, but there remained some unknowns. If a hydrogen atom contained 1 proton and 1 electron, and a helium atom contained 2 protons and 2 electrons, then scientists deduced that a helium atom should have twice the weight of a hydrogen atom. But this wasn't the case. Helium turned out to have *four* times the weight of hydrogen. A part was still missing from the jigsaw puzzle of the atom.

The missing subatomic particle was discovered in 1932 by an English scientist named James Chadwick (1891–1974). Chadwick proved that the nucleus of atoms also contains particles that have no electrical charge, and he labeled these particles *neutrons.* In the case of helium, its nucleus contains 2 protons and 2 neutrons, but hydrogen's nucleus contains a single proton and no neutrons. The two additional neutrons account for the fact that helium has four times the so-called *atomic weight* of hydrogen. Each element except hydrogen has neutrons in its nucleus.

Scientists later discovered that some elements can have varying numbers of neutrons in their nucleus. Uranium, for instance, can have 143 or 146 neutrons. By totaling the number of protons and neutrons in the nucleus of an atom, the atomic weight of an element is reached. Uranium that has 143 neutrons in its nucleus is uranium 235 (143 neutrons + 92 protons). Uranium with 146 neutrons in its nucleus is uranium 238 (146 + 92). These different forms of uranium are called *isotopes.* Each has slightly different atomic characteristics; uranium 235 (U-235) is better for nuclear fission than U-238.

DISCOVERING FISSION

While some scientists were busy unlocking the secrets of the structure of the atom, others were trying to learn more about the large amounts of energy that radioactive substances emitted. The energy in these substances wasn't released as fast as the energy released during the burning of wood or coal, but it lasted much longer and eventually produced more energy than any other kind of fuel.

Where did this energy come from? When alpha particles, which contained protons and neutrons, were released from the nucleus, energy was also released. Scientists thus reasoned that it was the energy that had held the protons and neutrons together in the nucleus of an atom that was freed.

Could this energy be put to use? The answer seemed dependent upon whether or not the release of the energy associated with radiation could be speeded up. The possibility of bombarding nuclei with neutrons and creating a so-called *chain reaction* that would speed up the release of energy was first envisioned by Leo Szilard (1889–1964), a Hungarian-born American scientist, in 1933.

The practical application of this theory was realized when scientists discovered that bombarding uranium with neutrons caused uranium atoms to split (or *fission*) into two elements with lower atomic numbers. At the same time a good deal of energy was given off. When the atom of uranium fissioned it released two or three neutrons that could strike other atoms of uranium. A chain reaction was thus started. The released neutrons would strike other uranium nuclei, which would fission into simpler elements and at the same time release more neutrons. And so the process continues. The neutrons emitted from the first nucleus strike two other uranium atoms, thus releasing neutrons from two nuclei and a good deal of the energy that had held the nucleus of the atom together. The neutrons released from these nuclei in turn strike the nuclei of four atoms, thus releasing neutrons from four nuclei. And so on in a geometric progression.

In 1942 a team of scientists led by the Italian physicist Enrico Fermi (1901–1954) built the first nuclear reactor

based on fission. This was done at the University of Chicago. The reactor was named the Chicago Pile One (or CP-1), and its construction marks the dawn of the nuclear age.

HOW RADIATION AFFECTS US

Why is radiation so dangerous to living creatures? The answer is that the energy released by radioactive materials can damage or destroy the cells of any animal that absorbs them. The particles of radiation do this by tearing electrons from the atoms within the cells, thus disrupting the chromosomes contained in the cell. There are forty-six chromosomes essential to the life of a human cell. The information contained within these chromosomes controls cell activities such as growth, reproduction, and the production of energy.

Two things can happen when a cell has been exposed to a strong enough dose of radiation. The cell can die, or the chromosomes of the cell can be damaged but the cell continues to live. If the radiation kills the cell or prevents it from reproducing, nothing adverse happens. Actually, this occurs every day, when we are exposed to cosmic radiation that the earth's atmosphere does not filter out. But sometimes cells that have been damaged by radiation are able to reproduce and create new cells, called *mutations*. These cells may be fine; in fact, some scientists believe that such mutations play an important role in the evolution of life on earth. However, these cells may instead be cancerous or abnormal and can cause death. Furthermore, if the damaged cells are part of the reproductive system, the defects may be passed on to the next generation.

Our bodies consist of many billions of cells. However, the injury from radiation to one cell can conceivably cause a cancer that may eventually affect the entire body. The amount of radiation the cell is exposed to and

Enrico Fermi

the length of time of the exposure determine whether a cell will be harmed.

One way scientists measure radiation is in *roentgens* (named after Wilhelm Roentgen, the discoverer of X rays). This unit indicates how many electrons are freed from atoms when radiation passes through air. However, the effect of radiation on living creatures is more difficult to calculate because several other variables must be taken into account, including the type of radiation (for example, X rays or gamma rays), the energy level of the radiation, and how far the radiation penetrates into the cellular structure. To account for all of these variables, another unit of measure was developed, the *rem*, which measures the amount of radiation exposure that a person has received. Rem stands for *roentgen equivalent man.* In most cases, 1 roentgen is equal to 1 rem.

Exposure to over 500 rem would result in immediate death for about fifty out of every hundred people. Even 250 rem would cause radiation sickness that would eventually result in the death of most people exposed to it. A hundred rem results in radiation sickness for most people. When the exposure to radiation is lower than this, the results are much more difficult to measure.[1]

As mentioned above, one important factor in how radiation affects a living organism is the type of radiation. It is important to note that radioactive isotopes have the same chemical characteristics as nonradioactive isotopes. Our bodies are basically chemical factories that process radioactive and nonradioactive isotopes in the same way. The byproducts of nuclear fission include radioactive isotopes of materials that the body normally uses. For instance, one byproduct of nuclear power plants is radioactive iodine (I-131). Because iodine is used by the thyroid gland, radioactive I-131 can become concentrated there. This is why some of the travelers returning from Chernobyl had radioactive concentrations of iodine in their thyroids. (See Chapter Five).

Some chemical elements are so similar in their basic nature that living cells may process both in the same manner. Potassium and cesium are examples of this.

Radioactive cesium is a byproduct of nuclear reactors. Potassium is an element that all the cells of our bodies need to continue living. But creatures exposed to radioactive cesium will process the cesium as if it were potassium and spread it to all parts of the body.[2]

How the radiation enters the body plays an important role in how severe the damage from radiation exposure will be. Radiation in the atmosphere that is absorbed by the layers of our skin will not affect our body's organs. An example of this kind of radiation exposure is sunburned skin. The layers of our skin have been overexposed to radiation from the sun, but our internal organs have been shielded. Radioactive materials that are swallowed or inhaled, say through contaminated drinking water or air, will have a greater effect on our body's organs because the body distributes the radiation throughout the bloodstream and the radioactive isotopes concentrate in the organs.

Several other factors can also influence how radiation affects a person. How old was the person who received the radiation? Was all or only part of the body exposed to the radiation?

The U.S. Environmental Protection Agency (EPA) has set the maximum allowable annual exposure to radiation at 25 millirems for all of the body except the thyroid gland, which can be exposed to 75 millirems.[3] (A millirem is a thousand times smaller than a rem.) At Chernobyl, the people living within 9 miles (15 km) of the reactor received doses of 10 to 45 rems. That is a thousand times higher than what the EPA says is a safe maximum. Using long-term studies of the effects of radiation on the people who survived the atomic bombs dropped on the Japanese cities of Nagasaki and Hiroshima in World War II, scientists have predicted that there will be between a 1.5 to 2.5 percent increase (about 350 people) in cancer deaths in the next seventy years amongst the people evacuated from Chernobyl.[4]

NUCLEAR REACTORS

3

HOW THEY WORK

How does a nuclear power plant generate electricity?

It all starts in the plant's nuclear reactor, where uranium fuel gives off heat through the process of fission. Water is piped past the fissioning uranium. Heat given off by the uranium changes the water to steam. The pressure of the steam is used to turn the blades of a turbine. The turbine powers a generator, and the generator creates electricity.

The technology to accomplish this process is very complex. The so-called *core*, or center portion, of the reactor contains as many as 40,000 *fuel rods* that house uranium fuel undergoing fission. To ensure that the fission in these fuel rods remains stable, a complex system of *control rods* are used to absorb the excess neutrons of the fission process. By absorbing these neutrons, the rods can control and almost stop the fissioning process. Depending on the temperature of the core, these control rods are pulled in and out of the reactor by motors.

One of the reactor rooms of the Chernobyl power plant. The reactor contains in its core rods of nuclear fuel like those shown below.

Some form of *coolant* is used to prevent the reactor's core from overheating. Water most often serves as the coolant, although some reactors use gas or other coolants such as liquid sodium. Many of the nuclear power plant accidents that have occurred are the result of a break in the flow of the coolant.

There is one additional complication. When fission occurs, the released neutrons travel at a very fast speed that must be slowed to ensure that controlled fission occurs. The control rods absorb neutrons, thus removing them from the fissioning process, but the rods aren't useful for slowing neutrons. To slow down the neutrons, reactors also contain *moderators* whose atoms collide with the traveling neutrons and help slow them down. In most nuclear reactors water serves this purpose also. Some nuclear reactors use graphite—for example, the reactor at Chernobyl.

In addition to the technology required for a nuclear reactor, there is the technology needed to prepare the uranium fuel used in the reactor. The steps involved in preparing the uranium are called collectively the *nuclear fuel cycle*.

THE NUCLEAR FUEL CYCLE
The uranium used in reactors is mined in far-flung corners of the world (Australia, South Africa, France, and the USSR). In the United States the majority of uranium is mined in the western states of Colorado, New Mexico, Wyoming, and Utah. At the mine, the uranium ore is crushed and ground (a process called *milling*) and then treated with chemicals. This is all done to extract the uranium ore from the rock in which it is found. After milling, the uranium is in a solid form—called *yellow cake*—that can be shipped.

Trains or trucks transport the yellow cake to processing plants that convert it into a gaseous state so that it can be enriched. Enrichment increases the proportion of uranium (U-235) that can be used as fuel.

Uranium occurs naturally in three atomic weights: U-234, U-235, and U-238. Over 99 percent of all uranium

Left: *a geologist uses a Geiger counter to search for uranium ore veins in Saskatchewan, Canada.* Below: *the uranium, after it is mined, is taken to a milling plant to be refined. Shown here are leaching tanks, where lime is added to help remove the impurities contained in the ore.*

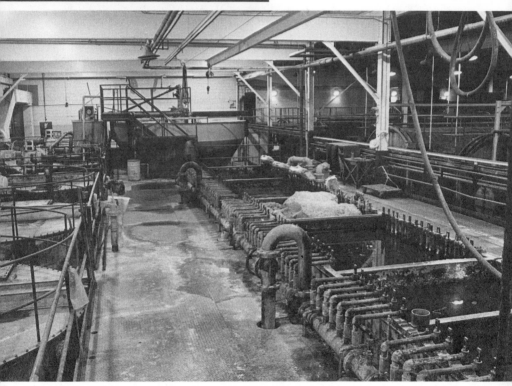

that is mined occurs as U-238, but it is only U-235 that efficiently undergoes fission when struck by neutrons. So the uranium is changed to a lighter, gaseous state, which makes it possible to concentrate small amounts of U-235 and create uranium fuel that is composed of 3 to 4 percent U-235.

Finally, the processing plant converts the enriched uranium gas back into solid form and packages it in the shape of pellets. These pellets are assembled into rods that become the fuel at the core of the nuclear reactor.

Eventually, after undergoing fission many times in the core of the reactor, the amount of the remaining U-235 in the pellet becomes too low for use as fuel. At this point the pellets contain mostly U-238, which doesn't fission effectively, and the byproducts of the U-235 that has fissioned. Technicians replace the used uranium pellets with fresh ones and remove the depleted pellets, storing them in a holding tank that contains water. Here the pellets cool.

Eventually, the depleted uranium pellets must be either reprocessed or stored in a permanent toxic waste repository. In the United States there are no reprocessing plants nor are there currently any permanent toxic waste repositories for spent nuclear fuel, although the National Waste Policy Act of 1982 mandated that there must be such a site in operation by the year 1998. In the meantime, spent uranium fuel is stored on site at each nuclear reactor plant.[1]

REACTOR TYPES

The basic principles behind the operation of a nuclear plant are the same everywhere, but the technologies that implement these principles vary. In the United States most reactors are either so-called *boiling-water reactors* or *pressurized-water reactors*. Both use water as a coolant. The boiling-water reactor circulates water directly from the core to the turbine. This means that radioactive steam turns the turbine, so the turbine must be shielded to prevent radiation leakage. The boiling-water reactor

A worker at the Tennessee Valley Authority (TVA) Sequoahyah nuclear power plant performs maintenance on the turbine blades belonging to the generator.

is the most commonly used reactor in the United States.[2]

The pressurized-water reactor has two water systems. The water pipes of the first system pass directly through the reactor's core and cool the uranium fuel. The heat is then transferred from the first system to a second system, in the process generating steam. In this way, the steam that turns the turbine is not radioactive. Companies in the United States manufacture both of these types of nuclear reactors, and plants based on these designs can be found in countries around the world.[3]

The boiling-water reactor and pressurized-water reactor are sometimes collectively called *light-water reactors* because they use normal water (called *light water* by physicists) as a coolant. Light water is ordinary water that can be found in our rivers and lakes. Another type of reactor is the *heavy-water reactor*, which uses heavy water as a coolant. Heavy water contains a special isotope of hydrogen called *deuterium*, which differs from other hydrogen atoms because it has a neutron in its nucleus. Ordinary hydrogen molecules have no neutrons in their nucleus, only a proton. The advantage of using heavy water is that it acts more effectively as a moderator. By increasing the effectiveness of the moderator, the uranium used as fuel in this type of plant does not have to be enriched to concentrate the U-235. However, because deuterium atoms occur only rarely, the heavy water must be produced. Canada uses heavy-water reactors.[4]

Some water-cooled reactors solve the problem of moderating the speed of the neutrons given off during the fission process by using a solid moderator, such as graphite, in the reactor's core. As we mentioned earlier, Chernobyl is an example of such a reactor.

The use of a graphite moderator is also common in a type of reactor called the *high-temperature gas reactor*. The operation of this reactor is similar to the pressurized-water reactor, but it uses a gas (such as helium) instead of water to cool the reactor's core. The high-temperature gas reactor has the advantage of being slightly more efficient than water-cooled reactors. Great Britain currently uses many high-temperature gas reactors.[5]

To this point, all the reactors discussed are known as *burner reactors*. This means that, figuratively speaking, the reactor burns up the uranium that is its fuel. In actuality, the uranium isn't burned up but is used until it can no longer effectively fission.

One problem with these reactors is that uranium is a limited resource. To prepare for the day when uranium is too expensive or rare to mine, the nuclear power industry has developed what is called the *breeder reactor*.

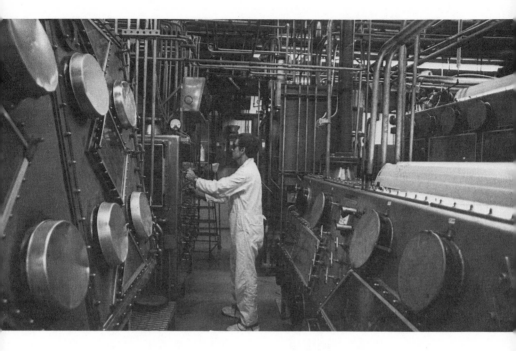

*A worker in a plant that processes plutonium
pellets for breeder reactors*

To understand a breeder reactor, you first must know that during the fissioning process several radioactive byproducts are produced, one of which is plutonium (Pu-239). Plutonium, which occurs only rarely in nature, is fissionable in the same way as U-235, so that it could serve as fuel for nuclear reactors if sufficient quantities of it could be produced. But burner reactors (such as the boiling-water or pressurized-water reactors) do not produce enough plutonium to be useful as a fuel. To produce useful quantities of plutonium the breeder reactor was developed. This kind of reactor transforms a higher percentage of its uranium fuel into plutonium.

Earlier, we discussed how moderators in nuclear reactors reduced the speed of the neutrons used for the fission process. The moderators were substances such as water or graphite. However, moderators do not slow down all the released neutrons. In fact, the creation of plutonium is dependent upon atoms of uranium 238 being struck by neutrons that have not been slowed down. The U-238 absorbs a neutron and becomes plutonium 239. This is the theory behind the breeder reactor, sometimes known as a *fast reactor.*

The breeder reactor has a different moderator than other types of reactors. In it, liquid sodium acts as both coolant and moderator. Liquid sodium slows down some of the neutrons but allows others to continue on at a faster, higher energy. These faster neutrons strike the uranium fuel pellets and transform some of the uranium atoms into plutonium. This process also occurs in reactors that use water as a moderator, but not frequently enough to produce useful amounts of plutonium. The plutonium can later be used as fuel for the reactor that bred it or it can be shipped to other reactors.

There are several problems associated with breeder reactors. First of all, in addition to being highly radioactive, plutonium is an extremely toxic substance. Because plutonium remains radioactive for many thousands of years, the processing and shipment of it between plants is extremely hazardous. Another problem is that the liquid sodium used as a coolant becomes a highly explosive substance if contaminated with water. This adds to the dangers involved in operating a plant. Finally, plutonium is used in the creation of nuclear arms. Many people fear that creating large amounts of it in breeder reactors will make it easier for terrorists to obtain it and build bombs.

Opposition to breeder reactors has stalled their development in the United States, although the U.S. Department of Energy operates an experimental breeder reactor in Idaho. But other countries have gone on to develop such plants. Both France and Britain have had breeder reactors in operation since the 1970s. Germany, in partnership with Belgium and the Netherlands, is in the process of developing a type of breeder reactor.[6] Unless the nuclear industry can develop a fusion reactor (see Chapter VII), which uses water instead of uranium as its fuel, it will eventually be forced to develop the breeder reactor to make better use of its fuel.

REACTOR SAFETY

The reactor accident that presents the most potential danger is a so-called *meltdown* of the reactor's core. If the radioactive byproducts of such an accident are released into the atmosphere, as happened at Chernobyl, radiation can be spread long distances.

The most common cause of a core meltdown is a loss of coolant to the reactor's core. One way that such an accident could happen is by the bursting of one of the pipes that carry coolant through the core. The coolant in these pipes is under great pressure and would quickly pour out of the cooling system, leaving the reactor core without coolant. Once this happens, temperatures within the core can rise dramatically. Eventually, the uranium fuel within the core would melt.

The primary safety feature built into reactors to prevent meltdowns due to a loss of coolant is an emergency core-cooling system. The backup system is designed to inject water into the core, thus keeping its temperature from rising.

Another safety feature of reactors are the control rods that are spread throughout the core. These rods are composed of materials (for example, cadmium) that readily absorb neutrons and thus help slow the fission process. In an emergency, the control rods can be jammed into the reactor's core, thus helping to slow the fission process by absorbing neutrons. This emergency procedure is called a *SCRAM*.

A final safety feature is the containment structure built around the reactor. First, the reactor core is encased in steel. The steel enclosing the core is also usually surrounded by a steel and concrete shell designed to contain any radioactive material that escapes the reactor.

*A nuclear reactor control room simulator,
used to train TVA's nuclear technicians*

REACTOR OPERATION

The personnel responsible for starting a SCRAM or activating the emergency core-cooling backup systems are the plant operators, who oversee the running of the reactor from the plant's control room. Aiding them in their job is a complex network of monitoring devices that record temperatures and pressures throughout the system. A typical control room contains large panels with hundreds of gauges and lights that give readings from locations all over the plant. Computers also provide the operators with information on the status of the plant.

Although training programs vary from country to country, all plant operators go through some kind of special training before being licensed for their job. Also, the operation of the reactor is governed by guidelines laid out by the engineers who designed the reactor. In the event of an emergency, the operators have special emergency procedures that instruct them on what to do. As the nuclear reactor accidents described in the upcoming chapters will show, the performance of plant operators is one of the most important factors to be examined in assessing nuclear accidents.

4

THREE MILE ISLAND

Prior to the nuclear reactor accident at Chernobyl, the accident that received the most publicity happened in the United States in March 1979 at Three Mile Island, which is 12 miles (19 km) from Harrisburg, the capital of the state of Pennsylvania and a city with a population of 80,000. This accident is especially useful to study because the chain of events leading up to it is so well documented. Although no one died at Three Mile Island, it had the potential for a major catastrophe.

REACTOR DESIGN
The reactors at Three Mile Island—there were two—were light-water reactors that each had two water cooling systems. The primary cooling loop was a closed system that directly cooled the reactor's core and transferred its heat—not its water—to the secondary cooling loop, which used the heat to generate steam that powered the plant's turbines.

The core: The core of each reactor contained 177 fuel assemblies that held about 90 tons of uranium dioxide

Three Mile Island nuclear power plant,
near Harrisburg, Pennsylvania

undergoing fission. Each fuel assembly was 10 inches (25 cm) square and 12 feet (3.6 m) long. Each assembly contained close to 200 zirconium alloy rods that held the enriched pellets of uranium dioxide. The fact that these rods contained zirconium became important as the accident developed.

The core also had slots for over a hundred boron control rods. The entire core was surrounded by an 8-inch (20-cm) -thick steel pressure vessel.[1]

The primary cooling loop: There were two primary cooling loops in each reactor. These two loops were identical to one another. Loss of coolant in one of these loops would eventually cause part of the core to melt.

Inside the primary cooling loop, distilled water was kept at a temperature of approximately 570° F (300° C). To prevent this water from boiling into steam, the pressure in the loop was kept at 2,200 pounds per square inch (psi). The pressure in a car tire is about 30 pounds psi. This water was constantly circulated throughout the cooling loops. It passed through the reactor's core, where it absorbed heat given off by uranium undergoing fission. After passing through the reactor core, the water exited through a pipe 3 feet (0.9 m) in diameter. This pipe carried the water to a steam generator, where its heat was transferred to a secondary cooling loop. Once the water in the primary loop cooled, it was cycled back to the reactor core through two large pipes. To force the primary coolant continuously through its loops, two large reactor coolant pumps were used.[2]

The pressurizer: The job of maintaining constant pressure within the primary cooling loops belonged to a large vessel called the pressurizer, which was connected to each loop by a pipe. Normally, water did not pass through the pipe. However, if the pressure dropped too low in a primary cooling loop, water was added from the pressurizer, thus increasing the pressure within the loop. If the pressure rose too high in a primary cooling loop, water from the loop was siphoned into the pressurizer, thus lowering the pressure in the loop. A pocket of steam at the top of the pressurizer controlled the water level in the pressurizer. Increasing the pressure of this pocket of steam forced water out of the pressurizer. Decreasing the pressure allowed water to enter the pressurizer. At the top of this vessel was a relief valve for the release of steam pressure, thus allowing more water to flow into the pressurizer. This relief valve played an important role in the accident at Three Mile Island.[3]

The secondary cooling loop: Water in the secondary cooling loop was turned into steam in the steam generator. This was done by passing the water over tubes that contained the much hotter water of the primary cooling

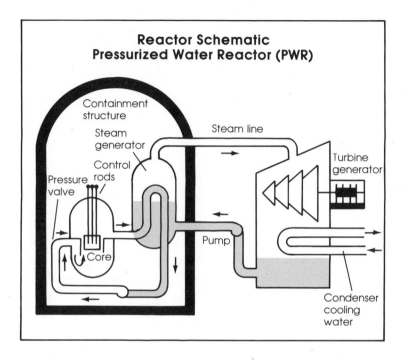

Reactor Schematic
Pressurized Water Reactor (PWR)

Containment structure

Steam generator

Control rods

Pressure valve

Core

Steam line

Turbine generator

Pump

Condenser cooling water

loop. From the steam generator the secondary cooling loop moved the steam to the steam turbine. The turbine turned the power generator, which created electricity. From the turbine the steam passed through a condenser that cooled it back into water so that it could again be cycled through the steam generator. When the coolant was returned to the steam generator, it passed through polishers that helped clean impurities from the water. This was the part of the system where the accident started.

The condenser: The condenser contained a third loop of water that did not come into direct contact with the steam of the secondary cooling loop. The condenser cooled the steam in the secondary cooling loop by absorbing its heat. The heated water in the condenser loop was cooled by passing though the plant's cooling towers, where it came into direct contact with the air.

The emergency core-cooling system: The purpose of this system was to provide a backup system for cooling the core. It had three major components. The first consisted of high-pressure injection pumps that injected water from a storage tank into the core. These pumps were designed to counteract any small leaks that might develop in the primary or secondary cooling loops. The second consisted of low-pressure injection pumps that could deliver larger amounts of water from storage tanks to the core. These pumps were designed to help if a large leak occurred in the primary or secondary cooling loops. The third consisted of core flood tanks that worked with the high- and low-pressure injection pumps in the event of a large coolant leak. If a large leak occurred, it would take a few seconds for the high- and low-pressure injection pumps to get water to the core. Those few seconds would be crucial because the temperature of the core would rise quickly. The core flood tanks, which were placed above the reactor, could dump thousands of gallons of water on the core immediately.[4]

The control room: Each reactor at Three Mile Island had a control room from which workers supervised the operation of the plant. The room contained a large control panel that showed temperature, water, and pressure levels throughout the plant. In addition, a computer system monitored many of the plant's components and provided printed data.

At the time of the accident, the control room held four workers. The operation crew consisted of two operators, a shift foreman for reactor 2 and a shift supervisor in charge of both reactors. All of these workers had extensive training.[5]

The containment building: Surrounding the core and the primary cooling loop was a containment building constructed of concrete walls 3 to 4 feet (0.9 to 1.2 m) thick. The purpose of this building was to stop accidental radiation emission from escaping the plant. One problem with the containment building was the large number of openings for water pipes and electrical wires. These openings allowed the leakage of small amounts of radiation.[6]

THE ACCIDENT

The first mishap: Early in the morning on March 28, 1978, a maintenance crew was cleaning the polishers in the secondary cooling loop of reactor number 2. On this day, reactor 1 was shut down for refueling, but reactor 2, where the accident occurred, was running at 97 percent of its capacity.

At thirty-six seconds past 4:00 A.M., the movement of water through the secondary cooling system stopped because of a blockage in the system's polishers. The maintenance crew had been removing resin-coated pellets from the polishers. The pellets absorbed unwanted minerals from the water. Cleaning them was a normal maintenance procedure that was done about once a month.

While the resin-coated pellets were being transferred out of the secondary cooling loop, the flow of water through the loop became blocked. This started a chain reaction that within seconds shut off the steam turbine and brought the flow of liquid in the secondary cooling loop to a complete halt. The primary result of this shutdown was that the secondary loop stopped absorbing heat from the primary cooling system. This caused the core temperature to quickly rise.

The plant operators in the control room did not at first realize that the secondary cooling loop was blocked. But after a few seconds had passed, the steam turbine "tripped" (shut off), and a light and a beeper (called an *annunciator*) warned them of the problem.

Two things should now have automatically happened in response to the problem. First, control rods should have fallen into the core of the reactor. This SCRAM procedure is meant to reduce the speed of the fission process in the core and thus the amount of heat produced. The SCRAM happened as it was supposed to, and within nine seconds, sixty-nine control rods fell into place. At the same time, the pressurizer's relief valve opened so that some of the pressure in the primary cooling loop could be released. When the pressure reached a safe level, the pressurizer's relief valve was supposed to automatically close. It didn't. The valve stuck open and steam continued to rush out the valve at a rate of 110,000 pounds (50,000 kg) per hour. This was approximately equal to losing 220 gallons (830 liters) of water a minute.

The second thing that was supposed to happen was that auxiliary feedwater pumps should have started pumping water to the secondary system. The auxiliary pumps started up as they were supposed to, but the operators failed to notice that the valves on the pipes leading to the auxiliary pumps were closed. (One indicator was obscured by a hanging caution tag; the other may have been obscured by an operator's body as he leaned over the panel.) This meant that they were unable to add water to the secondary system. Eight minutes passed before the operators noticed that the light indicators for these valves showed they were closed. At that time the valves were manually opened.[7]

Emergency systems: The plant operators were now playing a major role in the development of the accident. The operators had been instructed that the primary means for determining whether or not the reactor core was losing coolant was the water-level indicator in the pressurizer. As long as this showed a high level of water the operators were trained to believe that there was sufficient water in the primary cooling loop. The flaw in their training and with the written emergency procedures they were using was that no one had ever envisioned that the relief valve at the top of the pressurizer might accidentally remain stuck in the open position.[8]

As the pressure level in the primary cooling loop dropped, the emergency core-cooling system automatically turned on, and the high-pressure injection pumps pushed water into the primary loop. At this point the operators made a serious error in judgment. Seeing by the gauges that the pressurizer contained a high level of water, they believed that too much water was being added to the primary cooling loop. One thing their training had emphasized was that they shouldn't allow the pressurizer to fill completely with water. If that happened, they would lose the ability to regulate pressure in the system. To avoid this, they manually overrode the emergency core-cooling system and reduced the flow of water from the high-pressure injection pumps. What they didn't realize was that the water-level indicator in the pressurizer wasn't high because there was too much water in the system. It was high because water was flowing through the pressurizer and out the relief valve that was stuck open, into a coolant drain tank. The system was losing water fast. A loss-of-coolant accident was happening, but the operators believed just the opposite.

Two hours and eighteen minutes passed before the plant operators realized the relief valve was stuck open. Not until that time did they close it. Engineers would later speculate that if the relief valve had been left open another half hour to an hour, the core of the reactor might have been without coolant and could have completely melted down.

Hydrogen gas forms: Under normal conditions, the core of the reactor was covered by 6 feet (1.8 m) of water, but with the relief valve stuck open, this water slowly drained away. The temperature in the core rose faster, eventually topping 2,000° F (1,100° C). Some parts of the reactor heated up to 5,000° F (2,750° C), and the uranium fuel pellets began to melt.[9]

At the same time, a chemical reaction was taking place between the water turning to steam and the zirconium alloy of the fuel rods. The zirconium took the oxygen from the steam molecules and formed zirconium oxide. This process freed hydrogen from the steam molecules. Hydrogen gas is highly explosive.

During all of this, the operators believed the core was covered with water. The system pressure continued to be low, but the water level indicators for the pressurizer stayed high—a contradiction the operators were unable to explain.[10]

The public is notified: At about 7:00 A.M. that morning, three hours after the start of the accident, the plant supervisor notified authorities of the problem at Three Mile Island. They did this because shortly after seven, alarms went off that indicated a rise in radiation levels at the plant.

At 7:24 the power plant was put on General Emergency, a condition that meant that people living near the plant might be in danger of exposure to radiation. By this time, the radiation level in the containment building, which had been flooded with water leaking from the pressurizer, was averaging more than 1,000 millirems per hour. At a later investigation there would be a great deal of debate as to why the plant manager waited until then before notifying the authorities.[11]

At about this time plant workers began checking radiation levels outside the plant but found no increase in them. However, radiation levels in the plant's control room soon reached dangerous levels, and the workers put on face masks that filtered out radioactive particles. But the masks made it difficult for the operators to speak to one another.

During the rest of day one, communications with the Nuclear Regulatory Commission (NRC), the Department of Energy, and the Pennsylvania Bureau of Radiation Protection were established. The response of these government agencies was not coordinated and at times added to the confusion over what was happening.

At eleven that morning the plant supervisor ordered all nonessential employees out of the plant. By about two that afternoon, teams of government scientists had arrived in the area. The scientists detected no dangerous radioactive readings outside the plant. At the same time as government scientists arrived, newspaper and television reporters began flooding the area. Their reporting of the unfolding events added to the level of confusion.

*State officials notify the press of what
is happening at Three Mile Island.*

Instead of people being evacuated from the area, there was a large influx of scientists and reporters.

The danger of explosion increases: By 4:00 P.M., twelve hours after the accident started, plant personnel had correctly diagnosed the problem and used the high-pressure injection pumps to force additional water into the core and cool it. The danger of a core meltdown was now past.

However, there remained a dangerous buildup of hydrogen gas and radioactive material in the cooling system. The pockets of hydrogen presented a danger because of their explosive nature. If an explosion occurred, the radioactive materials in the cooling system (possibly in the core itself) would have been spewed into the atmosphere.[12]

On Thursday, day two of the accident, radiation readings were gathered by different teams of scientists. Government scientists recorded no dangerous levels of radioactivity near the plant.

By nightfall on Thursday, the influx of people into the area was making it increasingly difficult for government teams to coordinate their work, but the general consensus was that the danger had passed. Nevertheless, some residents of the area began leaving because of a television broadcast on the danger of exposure to low levels of radiation. Up to this point, no official evacuation had been started.

Inside the plant, operators continued to work on lowering the temperature of the reactor to save as much of the core as possible. Although the core was again covered with water, there remained the possibility that the hydrogen could explode. To lower the risk of an explosion, radioactive material was vented to an auxiliary building, and in the afternoon thousands of gallons of diluted radioactive water were released into the nearby Susquehanna River.

On Friday, day three of the accident, the venting of radioactive materials continued. The level of panic in the Harrisburg area peaked, and up to 40,000 people voluntarily began to leave the area.[13] The panic grew both because of the venting of radioactive materials and the continuing possibility of a hydrogen-related explosion. If such an explosion happened, dangerous radioactive materials would have been shot out of the plant. This was the kind of explosion that was believed to have partially ripped open the Chernobyl plant.

In the following days, the technicians reduced the amount of the hydrogen gas and steam within the containment vessel and the situation stabilized. Later investigations into the accident revealed that there had not been sufficient oxygen in the reactor vessel for the hydrogen to explode.[14]

THE CLEANUP

Once the reactor was stable, a long cleanup operation began. To accomplish the cleanup, special robots, sophisticated water-filtering equipment, and other methods for removing radioactive materials had to be developed. The reactor had to cool for three years before workers could even lower a remote-control camera into it. The entire cleanup will require at least ten years to complete. During that time millions of gallons of radioactive water will have been filtered and tons of debris trucked to a nuclear waste repository. The total cost of the cleanup is estimated to be approximately $1 billion.[15]

In summary, the accident at Three Mile Island was caused by a series of mechanical failures and operator mistakes. No one was exposed to lethal doses of radioactivity, but the level of radiation released by the accident was much greater than government standards allow. The effects of the low-level exposures to plant personnel are unknown.

An important second issue that arose during the crisis was the confusion over what government agency had responsibility for managing the accident. Lack of coordination between government agencies added to the level of confusion during the crisis. If a hydrogen explosion had occurred and a mass evacuation had been required, it seems doubtful that any of the involved government agencies could have handled the evacuation effectively. In addition, the large number of reporters that descended on the area increased the confusion and at times interfered with the work of government officials.

LONG-TERM CONSEQUENCES
OF THE ACCIDENT

The accident at Three Mile Island has resulted in long-term effects on many of the people living near the accident and on the nuclear power industry in general.

Testing of the people living near Three Mile Island has shown that many of them have developed mild cases of chronic stress. This type of stress has resulted from the uncertainty over whether it is safe to live near the reactors at Three Mile Island. Three years after the accident, psychologist Andrew Baum described the effects of the Three Mile Island accident this way:

> Three Mile Island is different than other disasters. When a tornado or earthquake occurs, the worst is usually over quickly. At Three Mile Island there is no clear sign that the worst is over.[16]

In other words, some people living near the Three Mile Island plant remained concerned about the possibility of another accident. Not every resident near the power plant has developed chronic stress symptoms; some show no signs of stress. But for those who have, psychologists believe it possible that some will develop physical problems associated with stress (high blood pressure, stroke, and other cardiovascular problems).[17]

One outcome of the psychological tests that were given has been that a citizens group, People Against Nuclear Energy, went to court and, using the test results, attempted to force the NRC to block the restarting of unit 1, the undamaged reactor, at Three Mile Island. (At the time of the accident in 1979, unit 1 was shut down for maintenance.) The courts ruled in favor of this action until October of 1985, when the Supreme Court overturned lower court rulings and allowed reactor number 1 to be restarted. Because of the lawsuit, unit 1 remained closed six and a half years; replacement power during that time cost the owners of the Three Mile Island plant slightly over $1 billion.[18]

The Three Mile Island accident has also affected the regulation of safety at other nuclear power plants in the United States. In particular, the accident resulted in more stringent requirements for emergency plans in the event of an accident.

For a power plant to receive an NRC operating license, it must now have emergency plans that pass federal inspection and can be tested regularly. The new regulations require nuclear power plants to provide a technical support center at the plant and an emergency

Many people living near the Three Mile Island nuclear plant continue to protest its reopening, even though it is years later.

operations center near the plant. The plant must also be prepared to make timely and accurate public announcements concerning emergencies at the plant. Backup communications systems must be maintained, and, finally, the power plant must give special emergency training to its personnel. For people living within a 10-mile (16-km) radius of the power plant, the company owning the plant must provide information on what to do in case of an emergency.[19]

In the event of an accident, the new regulations require that plant personnel first determine the level of danger. There are four official levels, ranging from Unusual Event, which indicates a potential plant emergency that public authorities must be notified of, to General Emergency, which means that there is the possibility of damage to the reactor's core and that the release of radiation from the plant will most likely exceed federal safety guidelines. In the case of a General Emergency, evacuation of all people within a 2-mile (3.2-km) radius of the plant is required. Evacuation of all people within a 5-mile (8-km) radius downwind of the plant is also required. Within fifteen minutes, all people closer than 10 miles (16 km) of the plant are to be notified.[20]

Although these new emergency plans have been criticized as not taking into account how people will behave in an emergency, they have already been used twice to successfully evacuate people in emergencies that didn't involve nuclear plants. In December 1982, 17,000 people were evacuated in two and a half hours from St. Charles Parish, Louisiana, when a chemical plant leaked toxic substances. The city used an evacuation plan drawn up for a nearby nuclear reactor. In July 1985, 10,000 people were evacuated from Cedar Rapids, Iowa, when a toxic cloud of gas was released from a fire at a sewage treatment plant. Again, the city used evacuation plans drawn up for a nearby nuclear plant.[21]

One outgrowth of the evacuation regulations is that they have allowed state and local governments to prevent the licensing of new nuclear power plants. This happened because the local governments must now approve of a plant's evacuation plans before the NRC can grant the plant an operating license. Such control of plants by states has effectively blocked the start-up of any new nuclear power plants in the United States.[22]

In February 1987, the NRC proposed eliminating the requirement that grants local governments this power. But this proposal has raised a good deal of protest among state governments, and if passed by the NRC's commissioners, it would likely result in Congress passing laws that would return this control to the states.

CHERNOBYL

The series of events that led to the Chernobyl nuclear accident occurred in quick succession, as is the case with most nuclear reactor accidents. The events that followed the mishap took longer to unfold.

The explosions that resulted in the release of radiation occurred on Saturday, April 26, 1986, at 1:23 A.M. A power surge within reactor unit number 4 caused the explosions. As part of a planned shutdown, the 1,000-megawatt reactor built in 1983 was generating a low output of 200 megawatts, but within ten seconds on this night the reactor's output soared from 6 percent of its capacity to 50 percent. Two explosions ripped huge chunks from the structure around the reactor and shot radioactive material out, starting more than thirty fires at the plant.[1]

The Chernobyl reactor operates on basically the same principles as all other reactors in the world. But the design of the Chernobyl reactor is a little different from that of most other reactors in the West.

The USSR already relies more heavily on nuclear energy than the United States and plans to have 50 percent

The arrow in this photograph points to the destroyed containment structure at Chernobyl after several explosions ripped it apart.

of its energy come from nuclear power by the year 2000. Ninety percent of the Soviet Union's fossil fuel stores come from Siberia, and it is very expensive to transport these fuels west to the European USSR. It is cheaper to use nuclear power there. Since the 1970s, the Russians have actively been developing nuclear power stations for this region. For example, the Ukraine, where Chernobyl is located, was getting 60 percent of its energy from nuclear power before the accident.[2]

It is not surprising that the USSR would turn to nuclear power to solve its energy needs. There is a good history of physics and nuclear science there and many prestigious nuclear research institutes. There are no formal licensing procedures for nuclear power stations in the USSR, and legal concerns are minor because nuclear power is not really under strict government control. It is controlled mostly by technologists. Finally, there is no antinuclear power movement in the USSR. Science and technology have been considered especially important to the economic health and growth of the Soviet Union from its beginning.[3]

Basically, there are two kinds of reactors used in the Soviet Union. The VVER (similar to our pressurized-water reactors) and the RBMK (the Chernobyl-type) reactors, as well as liquid metal fast-breeder reactors (of which there are currently two, but that number will soon be increased to four). The VVERs are popular in Eastern Europe, but there are difficulties in bringing them on line in a timely fashion. The Russians are looking into using prefabrication methods to speed up their development. This would be the first time mass-production techniques would be used in nuclear reactor design, but some Western experts are not convinced of the safety of these reactors. Many feel the Russians could be sacrificing safety concerns to meet target dates for nuclear power development in the USSR.[4]

The Soviet Union is the only country that has large graphite-moderated reactors. (The United States has one graphite-moderated reactor, a government-owned facility in Hanford, Washington. But this reactor's design is quite different from the Russian graphite reactors.[5]) The RBMK reactors have some undesirable features from a Western point of view. In 1975, the RBMK design was rejected by Britain for a number of safety reasons.[6] The Soviets do expect to eventually phase out the RBMKs, thereafter using reactors more like our pressurized-water reactors. But they are not planning to retrofit (significantly alter) the RBMK-style reactors, even in light of the Chernobyl accident, and are continuing to build and operate some of them, though with minor modifications to the system.[7] (We'll look at these modifications later.) In April 1987, however, the Soviets did announce that reactor units number 5 and 6 at Chernobyl are being canceled, though reactors 1 and 2 will continue to operate.[8]

RBMK REACTOR DESIGN

The general principle behind any nuclear reactor is almost as simple as that of putting a kettle of water above a flame. The fissioning (splitting) of uranium fuel gives off heat; water absorbs this heat and becomes steam; steam pressure powers a turbine engine; the turbine powers a generator that produces electricity.

In general terms, the accident at Chernobyl happened because a power surge caused a rupture in the pipes that carried water through the core. Without this water, the temperature inside the core began to climb dramatically. To lower the temperature, plant operators opened safety systems and dumped water on the core, but this resulted in the creation of steam under high pressure. The steam caused the explosions that ripped open the building enclosing the reactor.

The core: The core was placed in a concrete pit that measured 71 feet across and 83.5 feet deep (21.6 x 25.5 m). It had 1,693 fuel assemblies in the form of pressure tubes. Each of these pressure tubes contained a large number of fuel rods, perhaps as many as a hundred, and each fuel rod contained pellets of uranium. The pressure tubes were enclosed by 1,700 tons of graphite bricks, each about 10 inches (25 cm) wide by 10 inches long and 24 inches (60 cm) high. These blocks acted as a moderator (see below) within the core, slowing the speed of the neutrons that caused the fissioning to take place. Each graphite block had a hole at its center, and through this hole was passed a pressure tube.[9]

The pressure tubes were constructed of a zirconium alloy. Inside each tube, the uranium fuel rods were undergoing fission. Water was passed over the fuel rods, collecting the heat given off by the uranium. Each pressurized tube thus acted as a miniature nuclear reactor.

This design was thought to have two major advantages. First, the fuel inside the rods could be replaced

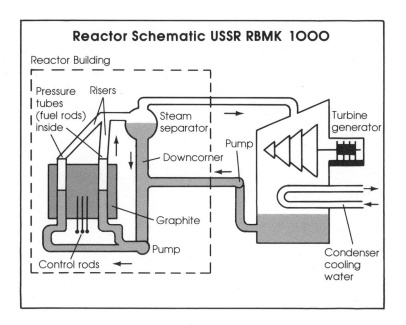

Reactor Schematic USSR RBMK 1000

Reactor Building

Pressure tubes (fuel rods) inside

Risers

Steam separator

Turbine generator

Pump

Downcorner

Graphite

Pump

Control rods

Condenser cooling water

without having to shut down the entire plant, as with other types of reactors. This resulted in an increase in the plant's efficiency. A second advantage that designers foresaw was increased safety in case of a loss-of-coolant accident. Because each of the pressure tubes received its own water supply, the designers reasoned that a single leak could not disable the system.[10]

The moderator: One way that Chernobyl varied from most reactors used in the West was the choice of graphite instead of water as a moderator. Graphite was chosen because it is a more efficient moderator. The uranium used in the reactor needs only to be enriched so that it contains 2 percent U-235. This is an important cost consideration. Boiling-water reactors require uranium fuel pellets that contain 3 to 4 percent U-235.

A problem connected with the graphite moderator is the high temperature at which it must be kept. During normal operation, the graphite has a temperature of 1,300 to 1,400° F (700 to 760° C).[11] This increases the

The turbine house of the Chernobyl power station

amount of heat contained within the core, which, in an emergency, places greater demands on the cooling systems. Since graphite is highly flammable, there is also the possibility that if temperatures rise high enough in the core, the graphite will burn.

The regular cooling system: Water cooled the Chernobyl reactors. It entered each of the pressure tubes from the bottom and circulated to the top, absorbing heat from the fission process along the way. At the top of the pressure tube, the heated water was removed and used to turn the plant's steam turbine. The reactor had two coolant loops that moved the water from the core to the turbines.

After passing through the turbine, the steam was

cycled through a condenser, where a coolant absorbed the steam's heat, turning it back into water. This water was then recycled back through the reactor's core.

The control rods: The reactor had 170 control rods made of boron carbide and clad in an aluminum alloy.[12] The purpose of these rods was to control the fissioning process in the reactor. Some of these rods were controlled manually by the operators; others had automatic controls designed to send the rods into the core when required. The majority of the rods had a length of 20 feet (6.2 m). The number of these rods that were to be inserted into the reactor was governed by written procedures, but the plant operators violated these rules.[13] One notable feature of the rods was that they had a slow reaction time, taking eighteen seconds to move from the full-out position to the full-in position.[14]

The emergency cooling system: Each of the reactor's cooling loops had an emergency backup system that had separate pumps to circulate water. The backup systems also had separate water tanks holding auxiliary coolant.

The confinement structure: Chernobyl had partial containment, which included separate structures around the reactor cooling pipes and water tanks that could withstand pressure of 66 pounds psi (4.5 atmospheres). The reactor and cooling loops were also surrounded by large buildings. This design represents an important difference between the Chernobyl and Three Mile Island reactors. The reactor at Three Mile Island had a large cement dome encasing the entire reactor and cooling system. The purpose of this dome was to *contain* the radiation in case of an accident. The reactor at Chernobyl had only a *confinement* structure that lightly shielded the separate elements of the system. Whether or not a stronger containment structure such as the one at Three Mile Island would have been able to withstand the explosions at Chernobyl is not known for sure, but many experts believe better containment would have prevented the huge release of radiation at Chernobyl as it did at Three Mile Island.[15]

The control room: The operation of the reactor was handled from a central control room that monitored the entire system. The room was filled with control panels that allowed the operators to take readings on pressure and water levels throughout the plant. Computers were also used to help monitor and run the plant. The training of plant operators and the written guidelines for operating the plant were the responsibility of the Soviet State Committee on Supervision of Safe Operation in Industry and Mining.[16]

The positive void coefficient: One additional design feature of the Chernobyl reactor, called the *positive void coefficient*, was a key factor in the accident that eventually destroyed reactor number 4.

Briefly stated, in reactors with a positive void coefficient, the rate of nuclear fission increases as the temperature of the reactor increases. One factor feeds the other in a vicious cycle. This dangerous situation can be triggered by a loss-of-coolant accident, which was what happened at Chernobyl.

Light-water reactors use their coolant as a moderator that helps slow the speed of neutrons within the core; this, in turn, allows the fission process to continue at a controlled rate. It also means that when a light-water reactor has a loss-of-coolant accident, it loses its moderator and the fission process slows.

The reverse can happen with a reactor that uses graphite as a moderator. When a loss-of-coolant accident occurs, the reactor still has the graphite moderator slowing neutrons and the fission process can continue giving off heat. At the same time, because of the loss of coolant, the temperature within the reactor rises faster. This, in turn, causes the fission process to speed up. As the accident at Chernobyl proved, this sequence of events can be very difficult to control.

The reason that the Chernobyl reactor was designed in this fashion was tied to the twofold use that the Soviets intended for it. In addition to generating power, the reactor was originally designed to produce weapons-grade plutonium. In order to produce and extract the plutonium efficiently, it was necessary to refuel the core without shutting down the plant. To accomplish this, the plant had to be designed in such a way that made a high positive void coefficient unavoidable.[17]

THE ACCIDENT[18]

On April 25, 1986, Chernobyl reactor number 4 was scheduled to be shut down to allow for routine maintenance. While the reactor was being shut down, plant operators decided to run a test on one of the generators. The purpose of this test was to determine how long the turbine powering the generators would continue to run and power the emergency cooling systems once cut off from the steam created by the reactor.

The emergency cooling system was normally powered by diesel engines, but it could take several seconds for these engines to start up and power the pumps that circulated coolant. During these few seconds, the temperature of the core could rise dramatically, and the only source of power for the emergency cooling system's pumps was from the power plant's turbine, which would eventually shut down because it was no longer receiving steam from the reactor. Thus, plant operators thought it important to learn how long the turbine could power the pumps.

Similar tests had been run before. This test was being run because a new voltage regulation system had been installed. During the running of the test, the operators violated several important safety rules, resulting in catastrophe.

At 1:00 A.M. on April 25, 1986, the first event in the accident occurred. For the purposes of the test, the power output of reactor number 4 was reduced slowly over a period of twelve hours from nearly 100 percent of capacity to 50 percent.

At 2:00 P.M., thirteen hours after the power output of the plant had been lowered, plant operators inactivated the emergency cooling system so that it would not start up automatically during the test. But before they could begin the turbine test, a local electricity dispatcher asked that they wait before lowering the plant's electrical output further. For the next nine hours the reactor was run without an operational emergency cooling system. This was one of a number of safety rules violated by the operators. In fact, this violation played no role in the accident, but it does indicate a lack of good judgment on the part of the operators. At some point during the long hours of waiting for the test to begin, the operators appear to have become more concerned with running the test and less concerned with the overall safety of the plant's operation.

At 11:10 P.M., the electricity dispatcher withdrew the request for electricity, and the operators continued with the test. The next step was to reduce the plant's power output from 50 percent of capacity to approximately 25 percent. In lowering the plant's output further, another operator error occurred that was responsible for disconnecting an automatic control system. The result of this mistake was that the reactor's output dropped to less than 1 percent of the plant's capacity.

In addition to the disconnected automatic control system, there was a buildup of xenon gas in the reactor. Xenon gas is a byproduct of the fission process, and it causes the chain reaction to slow. This increased the difficulty in boosting the plant's power output.

To raise the power output to the higher level required for their test, the operators withdrew manual control rods within the core. This was a further violation of safety rules, for the rods were needed to control the speed of the fission reactor. By pulling the rods, they were able to increase the power output to 6 percent of capacity but no higher, because of the xenon present.

It was now 1:00 A.M. on April 26, twenty-four hours after the shutdown of the plant had started. The operators continued to prepare for their test by connecting two pumps to the reactor. Because the reactor was at a low power output, adding water pumps to the reactor's cooling loop resulted in too much coolant flowing through the core. This caused the pressure and water level in the steam separators to drop and the reactor to produce less steam. If the levels in the steam separators fell below a designated point, the system would automatically shut down. To avoid this, the operators made another bad decision and blocked the signals from the sensors measuring these levels. This cut off an important part of the reactor's emergency shutdown system.

The decrease in steam generation also resulted in control rods being automatically withdrawn from the reactor. The operators had already withdrawn those control rods that could be controlled manually. At this point, nearly all control rods were withdrawn from the reactor. This made it very difficult for the operators to control the reactor.

At 1:22 A.M., the operators received a printout from a computer monitoring program indicating that the reactor should be shut down because of the inability of the operators to control the reaction. However, the operators delayed shutting down the reactor long enough to start the turbine test.

At 1:23 A.M., the operators started the test by shutting off the steam supply to the generator that powered the turbine. The generator, whose steam supply was cut off, also supplied power to four of the eight pumps sending coolant through the reactor. This resulted in a dangerous drop in the coolant level in the system. The coolant was rapidly turned into steam. Also, because of the positive void coefficient, the power output of the reactor began to rise quickly. The shift manager ordered an emergency shutdown of the plant. Operators attempted to reinsert the control rods into the reactor, but it couldn't be done in time. The power output from the reactor surged upward, superheating the coolant and greatly increasing the pressure within the reactor vessel.

At 1:24 A.M., an enormous explosion ripped apart the reactor and part of the building above it. Most of the top of the building was gone. A second explosion, which may have resulted from hydrogen released by the superheated steam coming into contact with the zirconium of the pressure tubes, did further damage to the buildings around the reactor. More than thirty fires started in and around the reactor building. The most dangerous of these fires was on a roof near reactor number 3, which was still operating.

COMBATTING THE BLAZE
Ninety minutes passed before fire fighters arrived to battle flames leaping as high as 100 feet (30 m). Two fire fighters died at the scene and 204 fire fighters and plant workers were later hospitalized. Dr. Robert Gale, an American physician and specialist in bone marrow transplants, flew to the Soviet Union on May 1 to help treat the Chernobyl victims. Dr. Gale said in a speech before the American Association for the Advancement of Science in February 1987 that he treated a total of about 500 patients with acute symptoms; most of them—460 or so—were already out of the hospital and doing well. About five were still in the hospital suffering from burns but were expected to recover. A total of thirty-one people died. Dr. Gale did only thirteen bone marrow transplants; most of the victims were saved by sophisticated blood transfusion techniques or antibiotics brought in from Europe and the United States. Many are left with severe radiation burns.

By 5 A.M., three and a half hours after the explosion, heroic firemen had the building fires under control, but the fire in the reactor core continued to burn. Fire departments as far away as Kiev, 70 miles (113 km) south of the plant, were summoned. Local police set up roadblocks that prevented people from getting within 10 miles (16 km) of the plant.

However, the Soviets knew that ordinary fire-fighting methods would never have been able to extinguish the fire at the core of the reactor. Pouring water on the burning graphite bricks would only have produced a flammable carbon monoxide that would have fueled the flames

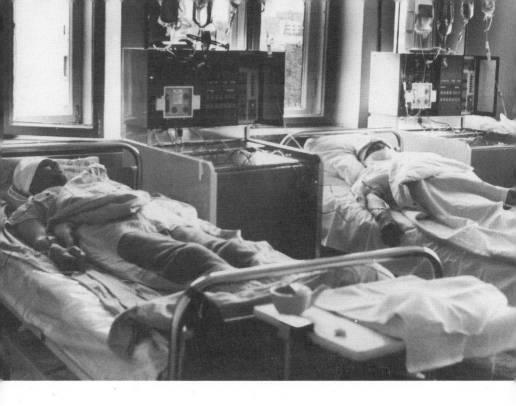

Above: *Chernobyl victims being treated with antibiotics.*
Below: *roadblocks sealed off Chernobyl. Here, vehicles leaving the area are checked for contamination.*

ЗАПРЕТНАЯ

more. Having failed on their own to extinguish the blaze, on Tuesday, April 29, four days after the explosion, Soviet officials sought advice from West Germany and Sweden on how to fight graphite fires. They were advised that to douse the fire, heavy-lift helicopters should fly directly over the open blaze and drop 5,000 tons of boron, limestone, sand, clay, and lead onto the fire. These materials would absorb neutrons freed during the fissioning process and absorb heat from the fire. They did this, and eventually the fissioning process slowed, the temperature dropped, and the fire was slowly extinguished.[19]

CONTAINING THE RADIATION[20]
The 5,000 tons of material dropped on the reactor core helped contain the radiation, but it also presented a problem. What if the structure of the reactor building could not support that much weight? In addition, there was still the threat of the superheated core burning its way through the bottom of the structure. To combat these dangers, workers tunneled under the plant and poured a layer of cement and boron beneath the burning reactor.

The possibility of a reactor core meltdown that burns its way into the earth has misleadingly become known as the "China syndrome." It gets this name from the idea that the core could burn completely through the earth to the other side of the world. (In the case of the United States, it once was a popular myth that if you dug through the center of the earth you came out in China.) Because the core would cool as it came into contact with the ground and thus would stop melting, the China syndrome could never happen. However, the burning core could come into contact with underground water and spread radioactive contamination throughout the region's water supply. This was why the workers put the layer of cement beneath the core. The cement was meant to prevent the core from sinking into the earth and to help encase it so that its radiation would be contained.

Rain posed another possible danger from the still-smoldering core. Runoff from a rainstorm would have washed radioactive particles into the Pripyat River, which runs near the plant. Fortunately, it did not rain. The Pripyat River is the major source of water to the city of Kiev. It flows through the city's reservoir and eventually into the Dnieper River, one of the longest rivers in Europe. To prevent the runoff from reaching the river when the snows melted, workers built a dike between the plant and the river. However, this will not prevent the runoff from seeping into the ground and reaching the groundwater.

Regardless of cleanup methods, land near the Chernobyl reactor may remain uninhabitable for many years. Although some of the radioactive materials that leaked from the reactor have a short half-life (for example, radioactive iodine stays radioactive for only a few weeks), others (such as cesium and strontium) may be a danger for decades. The half-life of a radioactive substance is the amount of time required for half of that substance to decay into another substance, which may also be radioactive. Some materials have half-lives that stretch over many centuries. Plutonium, a byproduct of the fissioning of uranium in nuclear reactors, has a half-life of 24,000 years!

EVACUATING THE PEOPLE NEAR CHERNOBYL[21]

At some time on Saturday, April 26, the day of the accident, evacuation plans were drawn up, and hundreds of buses began arriving in the nearby towns of Pripyat (pop. 45,000), about 1 to 2 miles (1.6 to 3.2 km) away, and Chernobyl (pop. 10,000), about 10 miles (16 km) to the southeast. While the buses were being readied, people were advised to stay in their homes. Because Pripyat is a high-rise city with concrete buildings, it made good sense to keep people at home with the windows closed until the buses could be assembled.

On Sunday, April 27, at 1:50 P.M., the evacuation of the nearby towns began. By this time the background radiation in these towns was as much as 50,000 times higher than normal background radiation. Over a thousand buses picked up approximately 49,000 people residing within 6.2 miles (10 km) of the plant. In a little over two hours only a few workers remained behind. Six days later, the evacuation zone was expanded to 19 miles (30 km) and an additional 43,000 people were evacuated, for a total of 92,000. In early June, 20,000 more were evacuated, due to "hot spots" that developed in the surrounding areas. All in all, more than 110,000 were evacuated.[22]

At this point, citizens of Poland and the Scandinavian countries were still unaware of the accident at Chernobyl. But the prevailing winds were already carrying radioactive materials toward them.

In Kiev, the third largest city in the USSR and only 70 miles (113 km) away, 2.5 million people continued on with life as usual. The sole indication of the nuclear power plant accident was disrupted bus schedules; this was the result of city buses helping to evacuate people from the immediate vicinity of the accident.

Foreign students and tourists in Kiev reported nothing out of the ordinary. Preparations for the annual May Day celebration, a holiday that honors international workers and the coming of spring, proceeded as usual. British students, who returned home shortly afterward, showed no signs of having inhaled or swallowed radioactive particles. Some of the British travelers had absorbed small amounts of radioactive substances in their thyroid glands, but physicians stated that the levels detected were not dangerous and were "almost comparable to normal background levels."[23] However, some students from the United States, who were in Kiev two days after the Chernobyl accident, had absorbed fifty times the amount of radiation given off by a chest X ray. Physicians felt that these students might have some long-term, though minor, health problems because of their exposure.[24]

JUST HOW MUCH RADIATION WAS RELEASED?

It is estimated that a total of 100 million curies of radiation were thrown off by the Chernobyl accident. Fifty million were in noble gases (rare gases that disperse quickly). A curie is a standard unit of measuring radioactivity.

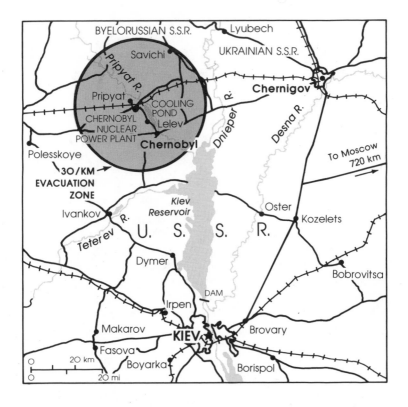

About a quarter of the total discharge of radiation occurred with the initial explosion, which threw debris 4,000 feet (1,200 m) into the air. Then there was a decline in radiation release, but after five or six days, there was a heating up of the reactor core and considerable additional releases of radiation lasting another nine or ten days. By the tenth day, May 13, releases were extremely minor. During this time, the Soviets were filling in the reactor's suppression pond with concrete, in preparation for dropping the dolomite, sand, and lead that would slow the nuclear reaction within the core and allow the fire to be put out.[25]

The worst previous nuclear reactor disaster, at Three Mile Island, released 17 million curies, but the containment of the accident was a *million* times more effective. Just 15 curies (15, not 15 million) were released into the surrounding atmosphere. The average dose of radiation for within a 6.2-mile (10-km) radius of Three Mile Island was 8 millirems. At Chernobyl, it was 40,000 millirems. Chernobyl represents the worst nuclear reactor accident to date.

AN INTERNATIONAL THREAT
What of the people beyond the evacuation area?

As the winds carried the emissions from Chernobyl to the north, rains deposited radioactive materials on Poland and the Scandinavian countries. Such radiation first appeared in the vegetation, particularly the grasses that drank up the rains. Milk from dairy cows that fed on these grasses was quickly banned in Poland and Scandinavia. The populace was warned not to drink rainwater or eat vegetables washed in rainwater. The Lapps, who had based their entire economy on the raising of reindeer, had to destroy hundreds of thousands of reindeer.[26] Other European countries banned fruits and vegetables coming from the Soviet Union. Children in Poland were given iodine to help prevent their bodies from absorbing radioactive iodine.[27]

In Sweden, radiation levels peaked at fifteen times normal. In Switzerland, levels reached readings four times higher, in Italy, two times higher.

Do these levels represent a danger? Physicians currently estimate that people in Scandinavia, where the levels were some of the highest, received the radioactive exposure equivalent to one or two chest X rays and should not experience problems because of it.[28]

On May 5, a week and a half after the accident, extremely small amounts of radioactivity from Chernobyl were measured in the western United States. Experts believe that these small amounts will have no measurable effects.

Above: in West Germany, a farmer disposes of contaminated lettuce. Below: in Lapland, herds of reindeer are destroyed.

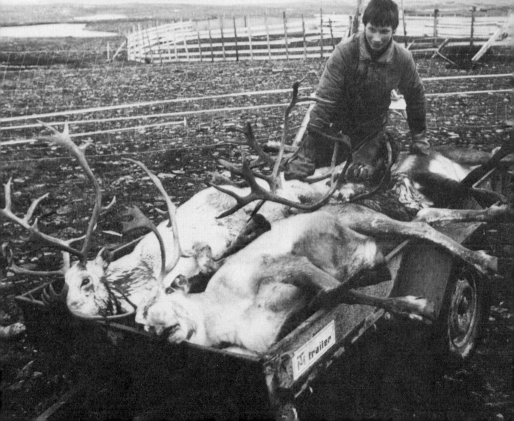

THE CLEANUP

The cleanup of the Chernobyl power plant will be costly and time-consuming. How long it takes will depend on the methods used. The cleanup of the Three Mile Island nuclear reactor accident, when finished, will have taken ten years to complete. This includes the time required to develop methods for removal of the radioactive core.

The first step in the cleanup of Chernobyl was the burying of the reactor in a cement tomb and the sealing off of the area. One important consideration in burying the reactor was the amount of heat that would continue to be given off for many years to come. Because of this heat, the cement tomb had to include a cooling system that could function for decades. Without such a system, the core could heat up again, causing another explosion and the release of more radioactive materials.

Another important consideration was what to do with the other three reactors at Chernobyl. These represented a large investment in terms of money, and they also generated a large amount of electricity needed by the surrounding area, particularly the metropolis of Kiev.

Whatever the Soviets do in addition to the initial entombment will require much more time and cost. To help determine what else needs to be done, remote-controlled robots have been used to survey the scene of the accident, take measurements of radiation, and complete some of the preliminary cleanup work.

The primary means of cleaning up nuclear reactor accidents has been to continuously flush the site of the accident with water. The water absorbs the radiation being emitted, and, as it is drained off, it is run through filters to remove radioactive particles. The length of time required to lower the radiation to a safe level, so that a person wearing protective gear can enter the site, is dependent on the amount of radiation released in the accident. A year passed at Three Mile Island before workers could reenter the building housing the reactor. Radiation at Chernobyl reached higher levels than at Three Mile Island.

Beyond washing the core with water, the Soviets will

have to deal with the structure surrounding the reactor. The cement walls and floors are covered with contaminated debris and imbedded with radioactive materials. High-powered sprays can wash off the dirt and dust, but special machines will have to be used to shave off the top layers of the concrete.

Once the radiation at the plant is lowered, workers can begin the job of disassembling the graphite blocks, metal fuel rods, and uranium fuel of the core. At Three Mile Island almost three years passed before workers were even able to view the melted fuel, which they did by inserting a camera through the top of the reactor. Finally, in 1985, five years after the accident, workers at Three Mile Island were able to begin breaking down the core and storing it in canisters. Workers wore protective clothing and stood on a stainless steel platform above the reactor. The core was covered by 20 feet (6 m) of shielding water. Through a slot in the platform, the workers manipulated clamps, grippers, or claws with 30-foot (9-m) handles. With these tools they deposited the melted core in the canisters that will eventually be removed and taken to a waste site in the state of Washington. If the Soviets decide to do this type of cleanup at Chernobyl, it will take many years to accomplish.

MEDICAL CONSEQUENCES OF CHERNOBYL

Only with the passage of time will the people evacuated from near the Chernobyl power plant and the citizens of Kiev learn if the radiation exposure has affected them. The Soviet government has released a report estimating that as many as 6,500 people may die from cancers caused by radiation leaked from Chernobyl.[29]

As mentioned earlier, the Chernobyl accident resulted in thirty-one fatalities. Two of these were not radiation related but rather the result of thermal burns and/or falling debris. The other twenty-nine deaths were caused by a combination of acute radiation exposure and thermal burns. Another two hundred or so persons were hospitalized for radiation injuries.

All the casualties were among the 444 plant workers, construction workers on the site at the time, or fire fighters and other emergency rescue workers who arrived soon after the accident. The workers who combated the fire received radiation doses in excess of 100 rem. Thirty-five people were exposed to more than 400 rem and a few received extremely large doses (1,200 to 1,300 rems). The deaths that occurred in the four months after the fire were from the group of people who received the highest doses. The Soviets estimated that people in the evacuation area received from 25 to 45 rems each. Among other possible medical consequences of heavy exposure to radiation are hypothyroidism, cataracts, sterility, cancer, birth defects, and genetic abnormalities.[30]

Dr. Robert Gale has estimated that ultimately there will be anywhere from 3,000 to 75,000 additional cancers worldwide as a result of Chernobyl, but probably the figure will be around 40,000. This will be in a population base of 600 million people dying from cancer over the next fifty years. One-third of these cancers will be leukemia, the rest solid tumor cancers. Most of the leukemias will occur within three to seven years. The other cancers will peak at thirty years, and most will occur in people who were children at the time of the accident.

Birth and genetic defects are harder to predict, but the Soviets are monitoring the situation. Of three hundred births the Soviets are following, twenty-six birth defect cases are expected to occur naturally, with thirteen additional victims possible because of Chernobyl. Genetic disorders occurring in victims may not be identifiable, as they usually show no symptoms.[31]

Attempting to put this in perspective, Dr. Gale stated that, in the same fifty-year period as 25,000 or so Soviets will die as a result of nuclear accidents (the rest will be non-Soviets), there will be 1 million lives lost in the Soviet Union due to fossil fuels, 4 million will die in car accidents, and 10 million will die from use of tobacco. This assumes, of course, that there are no more Chernobyls.

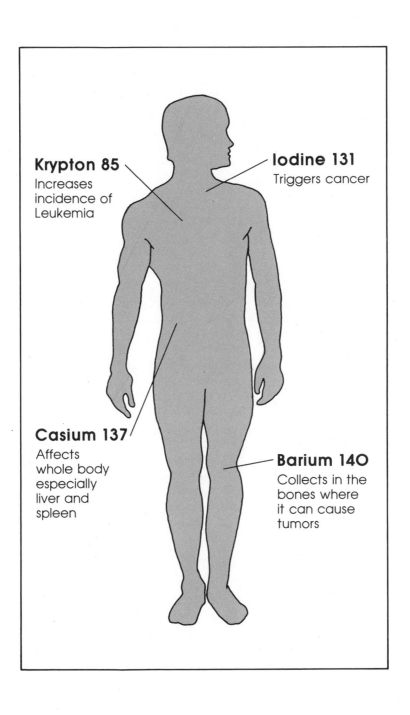

Krypton 85
Increases
incidence of
Leukemia

Iodine 131
Triggers cancer

Casium 137
Affects
whole body
especially
liver and
spleen

Barium 140
Collects in the
bones where
it can cause
tumors

THE SOVIET RESPONSE
TO CHERNOBYL

On an international level, the Soviet Union received stern criticism from other countries for not releasing information on the accident sooner and for not sharing more completely their knowledge of the events that led to the accident. In response to these criticisms, the Soviet Union retorted that the Western press had exaggerated the situation, and they agreed to fully inform the world of their investigation into the accident.

In May, under international pressure, the Soviets invited the International Atomic Energy Agency (IAEA), an organization associated with the United Nations, to visit Moscow to discuss the ongoing investigation of the Chernobyl accident. The IAEA inspects the reactors of participating countries. The agency's usual function is to monitor the plutonium produced by plants; it does not concern itself with the safety features of each plant. This task belongs to the regulatory agencies of each country.

Agency members flew in a helicopter over the Chernobyl site (the ground was still too radioactive to permit landing). In August the Soviets released to the IAEA a lengthy report that described in detail what happened at Chernobyl. The accident had occurred during a test, one of the purposes of which was (ironically) to find out whether greater safety could be achieved in the event of a loss of external power to the plant. The test was poorly written, it had not been well reviewed by their own in-plant authorities, and the person in charge of the test was not a reactor expert but a turbine-generator performance expert. Flagrant departures from normal safety procedures, probably done in order to prevent interference with normal operating schedules, had greatly contributed to the accident. The incorrect operation of the reactor was also given as the major cause of the accident, as were certain design flaws. For example, operators had been able to position some of the control rods farther away from the active zone than normal. It thus took them an abnormally long time to get the rods into the reactor when they were needed.[32]

The Soviets did not apologize for any of their actions or accept responsibility for any damage or injury to other countries. The Soviets said that no actual damage had been done outside their own country and that any agricultural losses by other countries had been self-inflicted. Since the Soviets signed no international agreements relating to this situation, it is unlikely that any other country will sue them in an attempt to recover damages.[33]

Immediately after the accident, the Soviets shut down twenty other nuclear plants that were similar in design to the Chernobyl reactor; these plants produce about 5 percent of the Soviet Union's electrical needs.[34] A short time later, however, the plants were reopened.

The Soviets have since announced some corrective actions they intend to take with all Chernobyl-type reactors. They will increase the U-235 content of the fuel, to make the void coefficient less positive, though this change will only be made as rapidly as the old fuel is used up. More immediately they will increase the number of control rods, position more of them nearer to the reactor, and add a lock on the mechanism that withdraws control rods from the reactor's core. They are considering adding a backup safety system and an improved shutdown system, and they will combine the three ministries currently in control of nuclear energy into a single ministry, called the Ministry of Atomic Power Engineering. Operator training will be increased, there will be greater monitoring of the main coolant pumps, and an effort will be made to use probabilistic risk assessment (PRA) studies—pioneered in the West—instead of the maximum credible disaster evaluations they had been using. With maximum credible disaster, engineers decide what is the worst-case failure likely to happen and try to design the reactor to withstand this kind of accident. With PRA, all likely accidents, or weak points in the system, are looked at. The Soviets will not change their containment, or confinement, design.[35]

The first and second units at Chernobyl are still working. Unit 3 was operating but was later closed down because of unsafe radiation levels. Construction of the fifth and sixth reactors at Chernobyl has been canceled.[36] The Soviets do plan to eventually phase out the RBMK-type of reactor, but only after they have lived out their useful lives. Six managers at the Chernobyl plant were removed from their positions and indicted for criminal negligence. They face almost certain conviction.

Before Chernobyl, the Soviet Union had fifty-one nuclear reactors in operation, which satisfied 11 percent of the country's electrical needs. They have thirty-two reactors under construction. Nuclear power is an important part of the Soviet drive to double the size of its economy, and Chernobyl has not deterred or even severely delayed this effort.

WORLD REACTIONS
TO CHERNOBYL[37]

Large-scale technologies are often viewed as infallible. Therefore, it is hardly surprising that the rest of the world initially reacted with great shock and fear over the situation at Chernobyl, especially since so little information on the accident was coming out of the Soviet Union.

The news media in the West, unable to get any hard information from reliable Russian sources, went with less reliable sources, and the result was a great deal of sensational reporting. United Press International, for example, reported a minimum of 2,000 deaths. U.S. officials added to the confusion by stating likely casualty figures in the case of a total meltdown. It was wrongfully stated by the press at first that Chernobyl had no containment structure at all. Satellite pictures showed the massive destruction and the reactor still burning, making it hard for Americans to believe the very low casualty figures coming out of Moscow.[38]

Moscow probably learned of the accident very shortly after it occurred but did not quickly inform the public, even the Russian public. This may have been because they just did not know how to deal with certain aspects of the accident.[39]

In the United States, there were few aftereffects from the accident, and there has been little change in policy because of the Chernobyl disaster. The United States currently has 93 nuclear power plants that produce 15 percent of its electrical needs. For many reasons (i.e., cost, safety, politics, disposal of wastes), no new nuclear power plants have been started in the United States for several years.[40]

In Western Europe, there was a widespread but short-lived surge of antinuclear opinion. Western Europe is highly dependent on nuclear power. About one-third of its energy comes from nuclear power plants.

In Britain, protestors demonstrated in the streets of London, demanding to know how many more accidents would be needed before the British government abandoned its pronuclear stance. But no changes would be forthcoming. Britain currently has thirty-eight nuclear plants in operation, producing 19 percent of the country's electricity.[41]

The reaction in France to Chernobyl was much less vocal. France has a policy of pursuing energy independence through nuclear power, and no large antinuclear movements flourish there. There are forty-three nuclear power plants in France that supply 65 percent of the country's energy needs. The French nuclear industry has one of the best records in the world in relation to nuclear accidents, partly because all of its nuclear plants are of the same design, thereby simplifying operation and maintenance. Canada, too, uses a single plant design and receives high ratings for safety. Canada has sixteen nuclear reactors that provide 13 percent of the country's electrical needs.[42]

Chernobyl did not appear to worry the people of Japan. China also said it planned to continue construction of nuclear power plants. By 1995 Japan hopes to receive 35 percent of its energy from nuclear plants. It also has a good record of nuclear safety, partly because of its tough inspection standards for its nuclear industry. Japan currently operates thirty-three reactors that supply 23 percent of the country's electrical needs.[43] It plans to put on-line 135 reactors by the year 2035. Much of South America, other parts of Asia, and Africa will also continue with their plans to build nuclear reactors. Like it or not, it appears as though we are going to live in a heavily nuclear world in the years to come.[44]

However, Chernobyl did lead to a reopening of the debate on nuclear power in Sweden. Sweden is the fourth biggest nuclear power in Europe, with twelve reactors. It had begun construction on a Chernobyl-like reactor, but work was halted because of the positive void coefficient problem. Sweden is currently considering the dismantling of other reactors under construction.

The examination of what happened in individual countries could go on. With the accident at Chernobyl's reactor number 4, the entire world had to consider the ramifications of nuclear power. Prior to this, nuclear accidents affected primarily the country where the power plant was located. But after the airborne spread of Chernobyl's radiation, citizens in almost every European country became aware that nuclear power plants beyond their own borders could be a danger to them. As a result, the debate concerning nuclear power was expanded to include international concerns.

The Swedish government demanded that Soviet nuclear power plants be subject to international control, and the West German government wanted experts from other countries to be allowed to visit the site of the accident. These requests may represent the first step in international safety regulations for nuclear power. At present, the only means of international control is the IAEA.

One result of the lack of cooperation between countries is that information and experience gained from operating nuclear power plants is not shared. The pooling of information about plant safety could do much to prevent nuclear accidents. For example, one of the reasons for the accident at Chernobyl was the lack of an adequate shutdown system, but Canada had learned this lesson in the early 1950s in an accident at its Chalk River reactor (see Chapter VI). Sharing such information could do much to prevent future accidents. Another benefit of an international safety agency would come from the inspection of power plants by impartial engineers who were not involved in the construction of the plant or the cost of operating it.

LESSONS LEARNED
FROM CHERNOBYL

Aside from adding to the dispute over continuing or abandoning nuclear power, the Chernobyl accident raised serious technical questions about the safety of specific nuclear power plant designs. In the West, because there are no reactors of the Chernobyl design, it was decided that an accident such as the one at Chernobyl is highly unlikely and therefore there is no reason for any change in U.S. regulations governing nuclear power plants.

In the search for new insights, Chernobyl has taught us several useful things. For one thing, we have learned that it is unwise to design a reactor so that safety systems can so easily be defeated. We must make our reactors more "foolproof."

Second, we now know that serious nuclear accidents can happen, and happen more frequently than were predicted. In the thirty years of nuclear power there have been three major accidents—Windscale in 1957, Three Mile Island in 1978, and Chernobyl in 1986. This is an average of about one every ten years. It is quite reasonable to assume, then, that the probability of another major accident in the next ten years is not less than 25 percent.

However, although severe accidents have been more frequent than expected, their consequences have been less severe than calculated. In other words, though we may be overestimating the infallibility of our safety systems, we may also be overestimating the risks.[45]

OTHER NUCLEAR
ACCIDENTS

CHALK RIVER, CANADA—
DECEMBER 12, 1952

The world's first nuclear reactor accident occurred on December 12, 1952. The reactor occupied a forested spot on the Ottawa River, which flows into the St. Lawrence Seaway in Montreal. The reactor was situated approximately 200 miles (320 km) upstream from Montreal, in northwest Ontario. The plant consisted of a hundred buildings and employed 1,500 people. Its primary objective was to produce radioactive materials, such as cobalt, which physicians use to treat cancer.

In the late afternoon a power surge occurred in the reactor. A plume of radioactive dust shot up through the reactor's smokestack and rained down on the surrounding buildings. Alarms sounded and an evacuation siren went off. To avoid inhaling radioactive dust, all of the 1,500 workers covered their noses with handkerchiefs and were evacuated on buses. A few scientists stayed behind to investigate the problem.

The report on the cause of the accident attributed it

to operator error in response to a reactor coolant leak. A technician opened several valves that should have remained closed. Almost 1 million gallons (3.9 million liters) of water were contaminated with radioactive particles.[1]

It took fourteen months to get the reactor back in working order. Decontamination involved draining off the million gallons of "hot" water and disposing of a 2.5-ton aluminum water tank that contained highly radioactive coolant used in the reactor. The hot water was siphoned out of the basement of the reactor through a pipeline that led to a remote area, where it was drained into the ground. The aluminum water tank was buried. Air within the plant had to be vented.

During the fourteen months of decontamination, technicians had to wash, sandblast, or grind surfaces that were contaminated. Radioactivity couldn't be removed from some surfaces, and these had to be shielded with concrete or metal. The technicians and engineers who did this work wore special protective clothing and masks.

Does this sound like a major accident? Yet no one was killed. Of the workers involved in decontaminating the plant, only one received slightly more than 15 roentgens of exposure to radiation during the entire fourteen months of cleanup. The medical officer overseeing the cleanup did not consider this a dangerous dosage, and none of the workers were reported as having any detectable aftereffects from their exposures.[2] However, note that the current U.S. standard for the largest annual safe dosage of radiation is 25 millirems. A millirem would be roughly equal to 1/1000 of a roentgen, so the worker received 600 times the dosage allowable by U.S. standards.

WINDSCALE, ENGLAND—
OCTOBER 7, 1957

The sole benefit of accidents at nuclear power plants is that they can result in improvement in the design and operation of other reactors. For example, the accident

*The Windscale atomic energy
plant in Great Britain*

that occurred at the Windscale plant eventually resulted in the redesign of temperature gauges inside reactors. Unfortunately, the British government later linked thirty-three deaths by cancer to this accident.[3] It is second only to Chernobyl in the amount of radiation leaked outside the plant—some 30,000 curies of radiation into the atmosphere. Chernobyl released 100 million curies and Three Mile Island 15 curies.[4]

The Windscale plant, located north of Liverpool, England, was an experimental station with a graphite moderator. (The same type of moderator was used in the Chernobyl reactor.) The accident happened while the plant operators were conducting a maintenance procedure that involved allowing the graphite moderator to heat up. The reason for this procedure was to release energy from the graphite blocks in the core. If the energy wasn't released in timed intervals, the graphite might eventually release its energy in a single uncontrollable burst of heat. The procedure had been successfully performed seven previous times, but this time trouble developed. The cause of the accident was eventually traced to the faulty placement of temperature indicators within the graphite blocks. Operators were unaware of the exact temperature within the reactor's core as the graphite was heated. The graphite became overheated and hot enough to cause some of the core's fuel rods to start burning.[5]

For two days the core of the reactor grew hotter without the technicians knowing its exact temperature. Finally, on October 10, operators discovered radiation spewing out a smokestack. The technicians first thought that one of the uranium fuel rods had burst and was leaking radiation. But when they donned white radiation suits and visually inspected the core, they discovered that parts of the uranium fuel were red-hot and burning.

To prevent the fire from spreading, the technicians removed the fuel rods nearest to the fire. At first, the operators tried to put out the fire with carbon dioxide. When this failed, they resorted to flooding the reactor with water. They had to flood the reactor for slightly more than thirty hours before the fire was extinguished.

—87

The fallout from the accident contaminated a 200-square-mile (518-sq km) area, and a radioactive cloud traveled as far as London, 250 miles (400 km) away, where radiation levels twenty times higher than normal background radiation were recorded. In Denmark, 500 miles (800 km) away, a slight increase in radiation was detected.[6]

People living near the Windscale plant were not notified of the emergency because officials feared they would panic. Readings in the vicinity of the power plant were over a hundred times the normal background radiation, but this was not a high enough level to cause immediate danger to the populace. Milk in the region was banned because it contained high levels of radiation which the cattle had absorbed from the grass they ate. Almost all of the radiation discovered was from radioactive iodine, which has a half-life of eight days. In a little over two weeks the milk ban was lifted.

An investigation of the accident stated that a lack of proper instrumentation and poor judgment by plant operators caused the fire. In future reactor designs, better temperature gauges were placed inside the graphite moderators.

BROWNS FERRY, ALABAMA— MARCH 22, 1975

At the Browns Ferry nuclear plant a fire came close to causing a loss-of-coolant accident. The plant is located in northern Alabama on the Tennessee River, near the town of Decatur, population 38,000. The plant had one control room for the two nuclear reactors that were in operation.

The fire started when two technicians attempted to seal air leaks in a room filled with electrical cables. This room was situated directly beneath the plant's control room. Electrical cables that came in and out of the room controlled many of the safety systems for the plant's two reactors. To seal the air leaks, workers packed foam rubber, which is a flammable substance, around where the cables entered the room.[7]

To test whether they had completely plugged an air leak, they held candles near the electrical cables. If there was still a leak, the breeze would cause the candle flame to flicker. The fire started when one of the workers held a candle too close to the foam rubber packing, which ignited. The fire quickly spread to the cables, and working along them, into the reactor building.

As it burned, the fire knocked out the primary core-cooling system and the emergency core-cooling system for reactor number 1. Without the water from these systems, the reactor began to boil away the coolant covering it. The water level within the reactor dropped from 11 feet (3.3 m) to 4 feet (1.2 m). To lower the heat within the reactors, SCRAM procedures were run. Plant operators were able to keep coolant circulating through the core of reactor number 1 only by attaching a supplemental pump to relief valves designed to release pressure from the core. Through these valves they were able to inject water into the core and prevent it from melting down.[8]

The fire continued for seven hours before it was brought under control. After the accident, the reactors were shut down for seventeen months for repairs. The repairs led the Nuclear Regulatory Commission to require expensive changes in other nuclear power plants.[9]

Several questions about reactor safety were raised by the fire at Browns Ferry. One concern was that the primary and emergency cooling systems could be disabled at the same time. This happened because cables controlling different systems were placed directly next to each other. When the fire started, it quickly spread from one cable to another.

The failure of these systems at the same time raised the question of quality assurance in the construction and inspection of nuclear reactors. Inspection of the reactors after the accident showed that fire safety should be an important consideration in the construction of reactors. Since the Browns Ferry accident, the Nuclear Regulatory Commission has required that electrical cables within nuclear plants be placed far enough apart to prevent fires from spreading from one cable to another.[10]

ADDITIONAL
NUCLEAR ACCIDENTS

The next two accidents do not directly involve a nuclear reactor but rather the transportation and processing of the uranium fuel used in nuclear reactors. Those who oppose nuclear power have long pointed out that the potential for lethal accidents exists within the entire fuel cycle of nuclear power.

The English Channel, off the coast of Belgium—August 25, 1984: The *Mont Louis*, a French ship, collided with a German passenger ferry and sank. Aboard the *Mont Louis* were 360 tons of uranium hexafluoride stored in sealed drums. The uranium hexafluoride was bound for the Soviet Union, where it was to be processed into nuclear fuel pellets and then returned to France for use in its nuclear reactors. Of the twenty-three crew members aboard the *Mont Louis*, none was trained in the handling of nuclear fuel.

The hexafluoride itself did not emit immediately dangerous levels of radiation. However, three barrels on the ship held uranium that had been partially processed. The contents of these barrels were much more hazardous than the unprocessed uranium. The danger was that if the uranium hexafluoride mixed with water it could explode, releasing the partially processed uranium into the sea.

To prevent the release of the hazardous portion of the shipment, a large floating crane was dispatched to the sunken ship. Scuba divers cut a 10-foot by 17-foot (3-m by 5-m) hole in the hull of the *Mont Louis*. Working with the crane, the divers retrieved the barrels of nuclear fuel from the ship. The cleanup took a month to accomplish.

At present, under International Maritime Organization rules, ships carrying 1,600 tons or less of nuclear fuel do not have to report to coastal authorities. In the case of the *Mont Louis*, the owner of the ship was reluctant to release information about the ship's cargo until forced into it by international pressure. As the nuclear power industry has grown, shipments of nuclear fuel over the oceans have also increased. The regulations governing these shipments are outdated, although the wreck of the *Mont Louis* has caused the International Maritime Organization to begin revising its rules.[11]

Gore, Oklahoma—January 4, 1986: This accident occurred at a uranium processing plant, killing one worker and sending more than a hundred local residents to hospitals for treatment.

The processing plant transformed milled uranium ("yellow cake") into a gas, which allowed the uranium to be enriched for use in reactors. Once turned into gas, it was shipped in cylinders to another plant, where the enrichment process took place.

The accident started with a stuck gauge that caused one of the storage cylinders to be overfilled with uranium hexafluoride gas. In an effort to force some of the gas back out of the container, workers heated the cylinder. This caused a small explosion that ruptured the cylinder and leaked a cloud of poisonous gas. The worker nearest the rupture was caught without a respirator on and was killed. Workers and people who lived near the plant were treated for inhalation of poison, plus skin and eye burns. No one else died from the accident.

Does this accident qualify as a nuclear accident? The single death was not related to radiation but to the inhalation of poisonous gas. There was no nuclear power plant involved. However, the processing plant was an intricate part of the nuclear power industry. In fact, the NRC had visited the plant just four months before the accident and cited fifteen minor violations of safety procedures. In particular, the NRC stated that the plant had to improve its handling of storage cylinders such as the one that eventually blew up.[12]

NUCLEAR REACTOR
ACCIDENTS AT SEA
At present there are over 350 nuclear-powered ships sailing the oceans. These ships include submarines, aircraft

carriers, freighters, and ice breakers that have been built by the United States, the Soviet Union, Britain, France, and China. They are built primarily by the navies of these countries, and because of the military connection, not a great deal of information is available to the public about the operation and accident rate of these ships. The advantage of adding nuclear power to navies is that the range of ships is greatly increased; for instance, some submarines could conceivably go thirteen years without refueling.[13]

The nuclear reactors used aboard ships are simply smaller versions of the commercial reactors. Ships' reactors are about one-twentieth the size of commercial land reactors, and because the crew of the ships live so close to the reactors, the reactors must also have better shielding than commercial reactors. In the United States, the reactors are built by the same corporations that construct most of the commercial land reactors (General Electric and Westinghouse). In fact, the commercial reactors were modeled after the U.S. Navy's reactors, which were developed first. Additionally, the work force at nuclear reactors in the United States is made up primarily of ex-navy personnel.

On the whole, it appears that nuclear-powered ships have better safety records than do commercial reactors, but there have been serious accidents, including the following.

The U.S.S. *Thresher*—April 10, 1963: The *Thresher*, a submarine in the U.S. Navy, imploded and sent 129 men to their death. It now lies in 8,400 feet (2,500 m) of water. The cause of the accident has never been made clear. The navy officially states that the nuclear reactor aboard the ship did not cause the accident. However, some navy experts believe that a ruptured seawater pipe spewed a high-pressure stream of water at the reactor's control board, resulting in a SCRAM of the reactor. This caused the submarine to lose power. It was already on a deep dive and without power couldn't stop the descent. It continued downward until reaching its "collapse depth." Fortunately, samples of the ship's debris indi-

—92

cated that only low amounts of radioactivity were released into the ocean.[14]

The accident points out a different sort of problem that ocean-going reactors have to contend with. Not only does the reactor have to function properly, but it also has to contend with accidents that can happen to the ship carrying it. In addition to the large number of natural dangers a ship has to contend with (such as storms, currents, and water depth), there are additional risks involved because of the duties of a navy ship. For instance, while testing the defenses of other countries, submarines in the U.S. Navy have in the past collided with submarines in the Soviet Union's navy.

The Soviet Union's *Lenin*—1966: The *Lenin* was a nuclear powered icebreaker that suffered a large radiation leak soon after refueling. Many crewmen may have suffered radiation exposure. The details of the accident are not

The Lenin, *the world's first atomic-powered icebreaker, experienced a serious radiation leak at sea.*

publicly known, but the ship lay idle for four years, until 1970, when it was put back into service with two new reactors.[15]

The U.S.S. *Scorpion*—May 27, 1968: The *Scorpion* was a submarine in the U.S. Navy that failed to reach port at Norfolk, Virginia. The last contact with the ship came on May 21, when it was located south of the Azores. The whereabouts of the ship was never discovered, so what happened to the ship remains unknown. The crew of ninety-nine died without leaving a trace. Possible reasons for the disaster include collision with another submarine; collision with an underwater mountain; a nuclear explosion in its reactor; and a broken seam on the ship's hull. The facts have never been uncovered. However, the navy points out that if a nuclear explosion had been the cause, they should have been able to detect the whereabouts of the ship by the radiation given off.[16]

Japan's *Mutsu*—1974: The *Mutsu* was a prototype nuclear cargo vessel belonging to the Japan Nuclear Ship Development Agency and was built for doing research. While on its trial runs, it developed a leak in its reactor's cooling system. The incident created a great deal of fear among Japanese fishermen that the ship would contaminate fishing grounds. The fishermen blockaded the ship with their vessels, refusing to allow it to dock. Eventually, the Japanese government agreed to abandon the *Mutsu*.

This incident raises an important question. How often do nuclear-powered ships accidentally release radioactive coolant into the water? Because of the secretive nature of the navies running these ships, little is known about such accidents, but several incidents have been recorded. In Guam, in November 1975, the U.S.S. *Proteus* released radioactive coolant into Apra Harbor. Some of the ship's crew maintained that readings of 100 millirem per hour were recorded at two public beaches near the harbor. In England in December 1971, the U.S.S. *Dace* spilled 500 gallons (1,900 liters) of reactor coolant into the Thames River. The navy stated that the coolant was harmless. Similar stories have often been reported in the shipyards where nuclear-powered ships are serviced.[17]

The U.S.S. *Puffer*—May, 1978: While the *U.S.S. Puffer* was undergoing maintenance procedures at the Puget Sound Naval Shipyard, coolant poured out of the nuclear reactor's system. The amount and level of radiation of this spill has been debated, but estimates ranged from 5 to 500 gallons (19 to 1,900 liters) of low to highly radioactive liquid. Also debated was whether or not the spill was contained or poured in Puget Sound. The navy maintains it was a small spill of radioactive coolant, but workers from the shipyard have publicly stated otherwise.[18]

The Soviet Union's submarine—October 1986: In this incident, a damaged Soviet nuclear submarine surfaced 550 miles (885 km) east of Bermuda in the Atlantic Ocean. An explosion aboard the ship had killed three members of the crew and ripped a hole in the top of the submarine, near a hatch that covered one of sixteen missiles aboard the ship. Each missile carried two nuclear warheads. The cause of the explosion was believed to have been a liquid fuel that was extremely volatile and stored for use in the missiles. The submarine attempted to return to a home port, but the damage was too complete, and the 120-member crew was evacuated to a Soviet merchant ship that had been helping to tow the sub. The ship sank to the ocean bottom, some 18,000 feet (5,500 m) deep at that location.[19]

The accident was not caused by the nuclear reactors aboard the ship, but here is another example of how problems on board a nuclear ship can cause a nuclear reactor to be scuttled. However, experts say there is no danger of the reactor contaminating the environment. Samples taken of air and water near the ship contained no dangerous levels of radiation, and the reactor was constructed using materials that would resist the corrosion of seawater. The reactor should stay safely settled at the bottom of the ocean.

7

ALTERNATIVE FUELS

Supporters of nuclear power do not argue that it is 100 percent safe. They acknowledge that accidents will happen in the running of nuclear reactors, but they counter that nuclear power is safer than other forms of energy. To support their belief, they point out the dangers associated with other types of fuel. This chapter provides a brief look at these dangers.

COAL
Mining coal is an extremely dangerous occupation. Cave-ins kill miners, and years of breathing in the coal dust found in mines can result in black lung, a fatal disease.

The mining of coal can also leave its mark on the environment. Underground coal mines can contaminate water supplies. Water that flows through abandoned mines reacts with the sulfur in the coal to form an acid that can then pollute other water sources. Surface mining of coal—known as strip mining—has often left the land unusable after the mining was done.

A coal yard and washing plant

The burning of coal also creates hazards. The primary problem concerns the sulfur oxide that coal combustion releases. The most disastrous incident related to this form of pollution happened in London in 1952 when a dense "killer smog" descended on the city, and the deaths of 4,000 people could be linked to the increase of sulfur oxide they were forced to breathe. The pollution came from the coal furnaces that heated the homes of London. This tragedy, along with others, was the impetus for the clean-air acts that many countries have instituted.[1]

Can these problems be solved? The answer is yes. Mining accidents could be reduced with better safety precautions. The environmental impact of mines can be reduced. Underground mines can be back-filled to prevent acid-water runoff; areas that have been strip-mined can be restored so that the land is usable again. Coal power plants can install systems (called scrubbers) that prevent the release of sulfur oxides into the air. Of course, much of this would be costly and would significantly raise the cost of energy.

OIL

Oil when burned for energy pollutes the environment, which in turn causes health hazards. The pollution starts with the transportation of oil. Because large tankers carry nearly 2 billion tons of oil each year, shipwrecks and oil spills are inevitable. Ocean-based oil wells add to the amount of pollutants in the ocean. Today, all of the earth's oceans have patches of oil tar in them that are the result of oil spills. The immediate effect of these heavy concentrations is the death of large populations of marine life. Even diluted quantities of oil are believed to have an adverse effect on marine life. But the problem is not limited to the oceans. Transportation of oil across fragile landscapes such as deserts or arctic areas also results in spills that affect the environment.[2]

Finally, air pollution results from the refining of oil and the burning of it—as gasoline—in cars. The end results of such pollution are difficult to measure, but it definitely adds to the smog hugging our cities and the acid rain affecting large parts of the world. Acid rain causes an increase in the acidity of land and water environments. This, in turn, has made it difficult for many species of fish to thrive. As the population of fish dwindles, so do the animals, such as birds, that feed on fish. Many lakes in northern European countries, such as Sweden, no longer contain fish. Environmentalists have long pointed out that destroying part of the food chain could eventually cause disaster for all of the earth's creatures.

Above: *an oil refinery in California.*
Below: *an oil spill off the coast of Brittany in France.*

NATURAL GAS

A fossil fuel that has some strong advantages over oil is natural gas. Its low level of impurities makes the processing of it cleaner and simpler than the processing of oil. But one problem with natural gas lies in transporting it. Many of the world's oil and natural gas fields are situated far away from the dense population centers that would consume it. The easiest way to transport it is through pipelines, but where large distances and bodies of water need to be crossed, this isn't feasible. An alternative method of transportation is to cool the gas and turn it into a liquid that can be transported. However, cooling the gas to $-256°$ F ($-160°$ C), the temperature at which it becomes a liquid, is expensive; and once stored in containers, it presents the risk of leaks. Such leaks could produce extremely explosive gas buildups. The end result of these difficulties is that many parts of the world, for example, the Middle East, continue to burn off natural gas rather than sell it. As with oil, improvement of technology can conserve and extend our reserves of natural gas.

SOLAR POWER

Solar power involves using fluid (usually water) to absorb the heat of the sun. Its application currently seems most feasible in the heating of houses. Energy collectors placed on a roof absorb the sun's heat, transfer it to the fluid, and pump the fluid throughout the house where the heat is dispersed. Several hundred households currently use solar power for all or part of their energy needs.

But the equipment to generate solar power is expensive to install, is not very cost effective, and presents hazards that need to be considered. Leakage of storage fluid can cause damage. Fires can be caused by overheating of units.

As a total answer to our energy needs, solar power doesn't appear adequate at present. It does appear that for small-scale applications it could replace some of the energy currently created by nuclear or fossil-burning plants.

WIND

Wind is one of the oldest energy forms people have harnessed. The Chinese built windmills as long ago as 3,000 B.C. Actually, wind power represents another form of solar power, for the sun causes wind by heating up large masses of air. The U.S. Department of Energy commissioned a study in 1980 that showed that wind was the energy source most able to supply electrical energy currently provided by nuclear power plants.[3]

Accidents that might result from large-scale wind power systems could include safety hazards for workers maintaining the tall towers required. Noise pollution could also be a problem. The environmental impact of massive systems of windmills is unknown.

BIOMASS

Another form of solar power, biomass refers to plants that have collected energy from the sun. The energy stored in these plants can be released by burning them (wood is an example), or by converting the plants or the wastes of animals who have fed on the plants into gases or liquids. The conversion of biomass into gases such as methane or liquids such as ethanol allows biomass energy to be more easily transported. If all the biomass available to the United States was funneled into energy, it has been estimated that it could supply 16 percent of our total energy needs. Sweden has predicted that by producing energy forests they could fulfill 20 percent of their energy needs.[4]

Several potential hazards exist with the use of biomass. Many of these are the same environmental problems associated with farming—soil erosion, depletion of water levels, and pollution by fertilizers and insecticides. In addition to these problems, there could be air and water pollution by the power plants either burning biomass or distilling it into a gas or liquid.

There are other potential energy sources, but, except for one, either not enough research has been done to estimate the liabilities involved with them (for example, the use of ocean waves to generate power), or else they are limited to use in certain locations, such as tapping the earth's heat near volcanoes or hot springs (called geothermal energy). One energy source that may offer large amounts of energy with low risk is another form of nuclear energy—fusion.

FUSION POWER

Supporters of nuclear power hope that a reactor that doesn't require uranium or plutonium can be developed. This type of reactor is the fusion reactor. It would work on exactly the opposite principle of a fission reactor. Instead of breaking down atoms, the fusion reactor would generate energy by combining atoms. Our sun and all other stars generate energy in this way. Two atoms of hydrogen collide and "fuse" to form a single, heavier atom of helium. When this happens, a great deal of energy is given off.

There are several benefits to a fusion reactor. First, for fuel it would use deuterium and tritium, isotopes of hydrogen that contain a neutron in their nucleus. These isotopes could be extracted from ordinary water, so fuel would be easy to obtain. The fusion reactor would not produce as many radioactive byproducts as a fission reactor, which would reduce the problems of handling and storing hazardous materials. Finally, the danger of a core meltdown would not exist with fusion.

At present, it is difficult to predict what kinds of hazards fusion reactors might pose. The reason for this is that no one yet knows how to build an effective fusion reactor. To force two atoms of hydrogen into one heavier atom of helium requires incredible amounts of heat and pressure. The temperature inside the sun is more than 36 million degrees F (20 million degrees C), but to create

*These giant lasers are used
for fusion energy research.*

fusion in a smaller space would require temperatures in excess of 180 million degrees F (100 million degrees C)! The problems in controlling such temperatures must be overcome before fusion reactors can become a reality. But if fusion reactors can be designed, they could provide energy for hundreds of millions of years.

At present, there are two basic areas of fusion research: laser-induced fusion and magnetic constriction. Each offers its own advantages and disadvantages.

8

HOW SAFE ARE WE?

This chapter summarizes why nuclear accidents happen, what can be done to prevent them, and how the handling of nuclear accidents could be improved. It also states the positions of the pro- and antinuclear groups over some of the many questions that nuclear accidents raise.

WHY DO NUCLEAR ACCIDENTS HAPPEN?

As the examples in the previous chapters showed, nuclear accidents have generally been caused by a combination of two different types of problems—mechanical failures and operator mistakes. In each accident discussed, both types of problems were present. Because they were so well publicized and have been written about so much, Three Mile Island and Chernobyl are good examples to use when summarizing the causes of reactor accidents.

The accident at Three Mile Island started with a small mechanical failure, the sticking of resin-coated pellets in a secondary cooling loop, causing the failure of a pump. The seriousness of this incident was compounded by operator errors such as turning off the emergency cooling system. Other mechanical problems—a valve stuck open—increased the danger. As precious minutes passed, the plant operators continued to incorrectly diagnose the problem and didn't realize that the reactor core was melting down. Eventually, the reactor was stabilized but not before coolant containing radioactive particles flooded part of the plant's containment vessel. The containment structure of the plant was strong enough to withstand the heat and pressure caused by the accident and prevent large-scale leaking of radioactive particles outside the plant.

The accident at Chernobyl started with operator errors. In order to run a test on a turbine, operators removed too many control rods from the reactor core. For the test, the operators also shut off the emergency cooling system and circumvented an emergency system that automatically shut down the reactor when pressure and water levels reached danger points. All of these factors combined with design flaws to make it extremely difficult to maintain reactor stability. When a power surge occurred because of the positive void coefficient (a result of the reactor's design), the operators lost control of the reactor, which soon didn't have enough coolant circulating through it to prevent the nuclear fission process from speeding up. Pressure and heat climbed rapidly, causing an explosion that destroyed the reactor core and ripped apart portions of the confinement building surrounding the reactor.

HOW CAN NUCLEAR ACCIDENTS BE PREVENTED?

Nuclear reactor accident prevention has two aspects. The first involves safety features related to the plant's construction. The second involves safety features related to the plant's operation.

Reactor construction: The reactor accidents that have happened during the short history of nuclear power have shown us that important design flaws exist in some reactors. For example, the placing of electrical cables too closely together, as in the Browns Ferry accident; or the lack of automatic shutdown systems if plant operators violate safety rules, as at Chernobyl. Some reactor accidents have resulted in improvements to the design of other reactors, but this has not always been the case. Changing the design of existing reactors can be prohibitively expensive, or at times the knowledge resulting from an accident has not been shared among different countries. This last concern—the sharing of accident information—is one area where an international organization such as the IAEA could play a constructive role.

In the United States, the NRC has the responsibility for the licensing of nuclear power plants and regulating the nuclear power industry. In practice, a power company applies for a permit to begin construction on a nuclear power plant. At this early stage, the company must provide information on how the plant will be designed, constructed, and operated. It must also provide an environmental impact study and preliminary evacuation plans for emergencies that might result from accidents at the plant. After examining these documents and any documents presented by groups opposing the construction of the nuclear reactor, the NRC decides if the building permit will be granted.

In addition to the design of a reactor, there is the question of how well the construction of the plant is carried out. A secondary question is how well the reactor is maintained. In the United States, the NRC is responsible for the inspection of the plant both as it is being constructed and after it begins operation. If the plant does not meet specifications, the NRC can refuse to license a nuclear plant for operation. More frequent and sterner inspections of nuclear plants can be costly, but they can also prevent mechanical failures such as the ones at Three Mile Island.

Reactor operation: Once the plant has been designed and constructed, the operation of the plant starts and a new variable enters in—the possibility of human error.

The people who operate nuclear power plants are required to go through special training. In the United States, to receive an operator's license from the NRC the new operators must pass an oral examination. Although the NRC handles the examination and licensing of potential operators, it does nothing to oversee the training of the operators. This has resulted in each power company training its own operators. Some schools that trainees attend have not been staffed by licensed operators, nor have the manuals they studied always been up-to-date and accurate.

But the most serious problem with plant operators relates to their handling of potential emergencies. Operators are trained to respond to emergencies by using special emergency procedures that have been written for them by engineers. Because few actual emergencies have occurred, the emergency procedures cannot possibly instruct the operators on how to handle every conceivable event during the emergency. Operators must make quick decisions based on the depth of knowledge they have about the reactors they control. Because of lack of experience and inadequacies in their education, not all operators have a complete understanding of a nuclear power plant.

Suggestions for improving the quality of operator training include more careful guidelines for the schools that instruct them and periodic inspection of the schools to ensure that training is adequate. Courses should be given on how to handle a variety of emergencies and how nuclear power plants operate. One useful tool in the training of operators could be the use of simulators that would allow students to experience staged emergencies. Such simulators are currently used to help train airline pilots to cope with emergencies. Finally, the licensing of operators should be more carefully supervised. Before being licensed, operators could be required to pass a test on a simulator that recreates an actual nuclear reactor accident.

Another operation problem is the design of the control room. During the accident at Three Mile Island, operators had to work with a control panel that was extremely complicated. As the tension of the emergency increased, the enormous number of flashing lights and ringing alarms made it difficult for the operators to understand exactly what was happening to the reactor. Another part of the control room that added to the operator's difficulties was the computer system that monitored portions of the plant. The computer printed all of its readings out on one printer, and as the number of pressure and water-level readings from different parts of the plant increased, the printer couldn't keep up and print the values fast enough. Improved design of the control room's computer system and control panel so that operators can quickly obtain the most important readings would increase plant safety.

INFORMING THE PUBLIC

There remains the question of how the public should be notified of nuclear accidents. After all, as shown at Chernobyl, the dangers of a nuclear accident can quickly spread beyond a power plant.

So far, we have two examples of nuclear accidents that resulted in evacuation. At Chernobyl, over 100,000 people were evacuated from the area near the accident. Although the evacuation appears to have been an orderly one, it didn't take place until thirty-six hours after the accident (see Chapter 5). At Three Mile Island, 40,000 people voluntarily evacuated themselves from the area even though no evacuation had been ordered. Their evacuation, which resulted from news coverage of the accident, was not orderly at all.

Although these two evacuations were quite different, there do appear to be some similarities between them. In fact, in each accident discussed in this book, the actions of people in charge of handling the accidents followed similar paths.

The most noticeable similarity was the reluctance of officials to announce that a nuclear reactor accident had occurred. There appear to be several reasons for the hesitation. At times it has been difficult to fully measure the dangers involved. Then, too, the persons responsible for first announcing the accident may also be the ones responsible for handling the accident. The demands of handling the emergency, perhaps coupled with a reluctance to admit that a mistake has been made, have helped postpone the announcement of reactor accidents. Because of the public debate over nuclear power, people in these positions may also want to avoid creating a panic if the accident can be brought under control.

A final reason that public notification has not always been timely is the question of who during an emergency is supposed to be in charge. The accident at Three Mile Island showed that government agencies were not prepared to deal effectively with the emergency, and the question of who was in charge was at times difficult to answer.

Several steps could be taken to improve the notification of the public in the event of a nuclear reactor accident. Explicit guidelines should be laid down for when such notification must occur. Who is responsible for making the public announcement should be clearly defined. People living near nuclear reactors should be educated on what they need to do in case of an emergency. Evacuation routes should be mapped out, and vehicles to be used should be designated.

NUCLEAR POWER:
FOR AND AGAINST
This section briefly sums up some of the pro- and antinuclear power positions.

In relation to general positions of the pro- and antinuclear groups:

Pronuclear: People in the pronuclear camp maintain that nuclear energy is the safest way to obtain the energy needed to run modern civilization. They admit that nuclear power plants offer risks, but they believe the risks to be lower than those involved with other fuels. The basis for this belief lies in statistics comparing the number of deaths from energy produced by nuclear power to the number of deaths from energy produced by fuels such as oil and coal.[1]

Antinuclear: Members of the antinuclear camp believe that the potential dangers of nuclear power are too great to continue using it. To support this assumption, they point to the hazards of radiation and the relatively high number of major nuclear accidents that have already occurred during the short history of nuclear power. They do not disagree with the pronuclear people about the dangers of other types of energy production, and they would like to see the safety features of other forms of energy production improved.[2]

In relation to the safety of the design and operation of nuclear power plants:

Pronuclear: In the United States, nuclear supporters argue that standards are stringent for design and operation, and that nuclear plants have more than adequate backup systems to handle even the most serious type of accident. On the question of Three Mile Island, they maintain that the reactor design succeeded in containing the accident and that not one fatality resulted from it.[3]

Antinuclear: When antinuclear groups discuss the safety of nuclear plants and the operation of these plants, they cite a growing list of accidents that have occurred at nuclear power plants. One of their primary concerns is that the NRC is not strict enough with the companies that own and operate reactors. In their opinion, the NRC has been too supportive of nuclear power companies and not critical enough of their faults. This is a criticism that antinuclear groups in many countries level at their government. To support their beliefs, antinuclear groups can draw on the testimony of ex-NRC inspectors and other experts in the field.[4]

In relation to the dangers of radiation given off by nuclear power plants:

Pronuclear: Supporters of nuclear power in the United States argue that the amount of radiation emitted by nuclear reactors is well below the guidelines established by the Environmental Protection Agency. They don't deny that there may be deaths should a major nuclear accident occur. Instead, they argue that people should compare the number of major nuclear accidents with the number of problems that constantly plague industries such as coal mining.[5]

Antinuclear: In addition to the large doses of radiation given off in the case of an accident like Chernobyl, antinuclear groups believe that the smaller doses of radiation that can be released by nuclear plants during normal operation are dangerous to workers. Their assertion is backed by scientists who believe that the long-term effects of low-level radiation exposure can result in diseases such as cancer. They acknowledge how difficult it is to prove such assertions, but there does appear to be a growing number of workers in the nuclear industry who are suffering from occupational diseases.[6]

In relation to the highly radioactive wastes that are generated by nuclear power plants:

Pronuclear: The main point that pronuclear groups make concerning waste disposal is that the amount of waste that nuclear power plants produce, though radioactive, is far less than the amount of hazardous (though nonradioactive) waste produced by fossil fuel plants. They argue that the small volume of radioactive wastes produced can be stored in deep underground sites where contact with water supplies is unlikely.

Containers used to transport uranium wastes
are shown here being tested for leaks.

Antinuclear: The antinuclear camp views the disposal of radioactive wastes as a costly and difficult undertaking. They don't dispute that the volume of waste is small when compared to coal plants, but they believe that volume is not important when discussing the wastes generated by nuclear plants because even tiny amounts of radioactive waste are extremely dangerous. In addition, the long half-lives of the radioactive byproducts of nuclear reactors will require storage facilities that are foolproof for many centuries.

Both pro- and antinuclear groups agree that a serious problem will soon exist in the United States because there is currently no long-term storage site for reactor byproducts. In 1982, the U.S. Congress passed the Nuclear

Waste Policy Act that called for the building of two permanent repositories for nuclear fuel, but little has been done thus far to make these a reality. As of 1982, there were 8,800 tons of spent uranium fuel in the United States; the fuel was being temporarily stored in water tanks. By the year 2000 it is estimated that the amount of radioactive waste will be 86,900 tons. The two repositories, when they are finally built, will be situated 2,000 to 4,000 feet (600 to 1,200 m) underground. The sites picked will be stable rock formations that can hold the waste for 10,000 years.[7]

The transportation of nuclear wastes to storage sites is also a problem. Antinuclear groups are concerned about the possibility of accidents. If such an accident occurs, serious contamination could result.

In relation to whether nuclear power is the cheapest way to produce electricity:

Pronuclear: When nuclear power was first developed, its supporters believed it would be the cheapest way to generate electricity. Some suggested that it would be so cheap that it could be given away for free! However, because of the high costs of constructing reactors, mining uranium, and taking additional safety measures to comply with increased government regulation, this has not proved to be true. Instead of emphasizing the cost benefits of nuclear power, its supporters point out that it is comparable in cost to coal, and that a country needs to have diverse forms of energy. They contend that countries without different forms of generating power will become dependent upon other countries for their energy needs.[8]

One criticism that supporters of nuclear power must frequently face is the fact that governments spend billions of dollars to support nuclear research. Pronuclear groups believe it a good investment and point out that in the United States the government helps a large number of industries with price supports and bailouts.

Antinuclear: Foes of nuclear power list several factors that have made it an expensive source of energy. The construction costs of nuclear plants have risen sharply because the demand for improved safety requirements have made construction more complex. Another criticism by antinuclear groups is that nuclear plants rarely produce at their full capacity because of the amount of time they are shut down for maintenance and refueling. A report published by a group called the Business and Professional People for the Public Interest stated that nuclear reactors ran at 55.2 percent capacity, compared to 68.9 percent capacity for fossil fuel plants.[9]

Another cost consideration is the expense of repairing reactors after nuclear accidents. Repair costs are higher for nuclear reactors than for fossil fuel plants, partly because of methods used to protect workers from the danger of radiation exposure. Also, the cost of replacement power while nuclear plants are being repaired adds to the expense of nuclear power. In the case of the Browns Ferry reactor accident, replacement power cost $5 million a month for over a year.[10]

Estimating the cost of disposing of hazardous wastes produced by nuclear plants is difficult, but antinuclear groups assert that it will be very expensive. Finally, the cost of uranium has risen sharply in recent years. In the early 1970s, the cost of uranium was $6 per pound, but by the end of the 1970s it had risen to over $50 per pound.[11]

NUCLEAR POWER IN SUMMARY

Nuclear accidents appear to be an inevitable fact of operating nuclear power plants. Those who support nuclear power believe that the likelihood of major accidents and the ill effects of radiation exposure have been overdramatized. Their concern is that without nuclear power the world will soon run out of energy resources. Those who oppose nuclear power believe the opposite, that radiation presents a dangerous threat to the environment and that major accidents will occur at nuclear power plants that will release this deadly radiation.

The reaction to the accident at Chernobyl has strengthened the position of antinuclear groups in Scandinavian countries and postponed indefinitely the building of some nuclear power plants there. However, the Chernobyl accident has not affected the pronuclear stance of countries such as the Soviet Union, Britain, Japan, and France.

Regardless of what decision is made about nuclear power in the future, there is still the question of the nuclear reactors that are already in operation. What can be done to improve the safety of these plants?

First, the quality of training for the operators who run the plants could be improved. Second, design improvements could make the plants safer. For example, most plants in the United States were designed in the 1960s, and much has been learned about nuclear reactors since then. Third, sterner inspections of plants might help prevent the malfunction of equipment. Fourth, better plans for handling nuclear accidents need to be developed. The one thing that previous nuclear accidents have proven is that both the personnel at power plants and the people who live near the plants have been unprepared to deal with emergencies.

No energy source is risk free. Of all the problems posed by modern civilization, the question of where we will get our energy from is one of the most basic. How we answer it may be crucial.

NOTES

CHAPTER 1
1. IAEA "Perhaps the Worst, Not the First," *Time,* 12 May 1986, 50.
2. Abigail Trafford and Stanley Wellborn, "Stark Fallout," *U.S. News & World Report,* 12 May 1986, 20.
3. David M. Gates, *Energy and Ecology* (Sunderland, MA: Sinauer Publishers, Inc., 1985), 64-6.
4. Joyce Barnathan and Steven Strasser, "Meltdown," *Newsweek,* 12 May 1986, 24.
5. Ingemar Lindahl, "The Geopolitical Dimension." Speech delivered to the 1987 annual meeting of the American Association for the Advancement of Science (AAAS), February 1987, in Chicago, Illinois.
6. "Deadly Meltdown," *Time,* 12 May 1986, 39.

CHAPTER 2
1. Gates, *Energy and Ecology,* 319.
2. John Gofman and Arthur Tamplin, *Poisoned Power* (Emmaus, PA: Rodale Press, 1971), 53-4.
3. "Protection of Environment," Code of Federal Regulations, Vol. 40 (1986), 7.
4. Simon Rippon, "Chernobyl: The Soviet Report," *Nuclear News,* October 1986, 66.

CHAPTER 3
1. "Too Hot for the Usual Burial," *Time,* 10 January 1983, 19.

2. John Abbots and Ralph Nader, *The Menace of Atomic Energy* (New York: W.W. Norton & Co., 1977), 306.
3. Ibid., 43.
4. Gates, *Energy and Ecology*, 299.
5. Ibid.
6. Walter Patterson, "Breeder Reactor Politics in Europe," *Bulletin of the Atomic Scientist* (May 1986), 38.

CHAPTER 4
1. Daniel Martin, *Three Mile Island* (Cambridge, MA: Ballinger Publishing Company, 1980), 13-14.
2. Mitchell Rogovin, *Three Mile Island: A Report to the Commissioners and to the Public* (Nuclear Regulatory Commission Special Inquiry Group, 1980), 10.
3. Ibid., 11.
4. Ibid., 12.
5. Ibid., 11.
6. Daniel Martin, *Three Mile Island*, 61.
7. Mark Stephens, *Three Mile Island, The Hour-by-Hour Account of What Really Happened* (New York: Random House, 1980), 10-12.
8. Rogovin, *Three Mile Island*, 16.
9. Stephens, *Three Mile Island*, 20.
10. Ibid., 21.
11. Ibid., 48.
12. Ibid., 178.
13. Ibid., 174.
14. "TMI—Technical Blow by Blow," IEEE *Spectrum Magazine*, Nov. 1979.
15. William Marbach, "Cleaning Up the Mess," *Newsweek*, 12 May 1986, 31.
16. W. Herbert, "TMI Uncertainty Is Causing Chronic Stress," *Science News*, 8 May 1982, 308.
17. Ibid.
18. "TMI-1 Restart Underway," *Science News*, 12 October 1985, 229.
19. "Emergency Planning," Public Affairs and Information Program, Atomic Industrial Forum, Inc. (July 1986), 1-2.
20. Ibid., 2.
21. Ibid., 3.
22. J. Raloff, "Controversy Over Nuclear Evacuation Planning," *Science News*, 14 February 1987, 100.

CHAPTER 5
1. Rippon, "Chernobyl: The Soviet Report," 59-62.
2. Paul Josephson, "The Historical Roots of Chernobyl," Speech given to the 1987 annual meeting of the American Association for the Advancement of Science (AAAS), February 1987, in Chicago, Illinois.

3. Ibid.
4. Ibid.
5. Andrea Gabor, "Thinking the Unthinkable: Can It Happen Here?" *U. S. News & World Report*, 12 May 1986, 22.
6. Peter Potter, "RBMK 1000—What the British Thought," *Nuclear Engineering International* (June 1986), 14.
7. Miles Leverett, "Chernobyl: Lessons for U.S. Science and Technology," Speech given to the 1987 annual meeting of the American Association for the Advancement of Science (AAAS), February 1987, in Chicago, Illinois.
8. "2 Reactors Are Canceled," *The New York Times*, 26 April 1987, Sec. 1, 16.
9. "RBMK 1000 Design," *Nuclear Engineering International* (June 1987), 7.
10. N.A. Dollezhal, "Graphite-water Steam-generating Reactors in the U.S.S.R.," *Nuclear Energy* (October 1981), 385.
11. Rippon, "Chernobyl: The Soviet Report," 64.
12. "RBMK 1000 Design," 7.
13. Rippon, 60.
14. Leverett, AAAS speech.
15. Rippon, 60.
16. B.A. Semenov, "Nuclear Power in the Soviet Union," *IAEA Bulletin*, Vol. 25, No. 2, 53.
17. William Reinhardt, "Soviet Reactor Was Flawed," *Engineering News Record*, 30 May 1986, 16.
18. Rippon, 59-60.
19. Colin Norman, "Chernobyl: Errors and Design Flaws," *Science*, 5 September 1986, 233.
20. William Chase, "Chernobyl's Fiery Story Emerges," *U.S. News & World Report*, 19 May 1986, 23.
21. Robert Gale, M.D., "The Medical Consequences of Chernobyl," Speech given to the annual meeting of the American Association for the Advancement of Science (AAAS), February 1987, in Chicago, Illinois.
22. Herbert L. Adams, "How Radiation Victims Suffer," *Bulletin of Atomic Scientists* (August/September 1986).
23. Barnathan and Strassen, "Meltdown," 30.
24. John Greenwald, "More Fallout from Chernobyl," *Time*, 19 May 1986, 44.
25. Gale, AAAS speech.
26. "Chernobyl: New Estimates of Deaths, Concerns for the Food Chain," *Environment* (September 1986), 22.
27. Greenwald, "More Fallout from Chernobyl," 44; Barnathan and Strasser, 24.
28. Colin Norman and David Dickson, "The Aftermath of Chernobyl," *Science*, 12 September 1986, 1142.
29. "The Chernobyl Accident and Consequences," Public Affairs and Information Program, Atomic Industrial Forum, Inc. (July 1986), 3.

30. Gale, AAAS speech.
31. Ibid.
32. Leverett, AAAS speech.
33. Lindahl, AAAS speech.
34. Greenwald, 50.
35. "The Chernobyl Accident and Consequences," Public Affairs and Information Program, 3.
36. "2 Reactors Are Canceled," 16.
37. Greenwald, 43.
38. Bill Kurtis, "Reporting the News from Chernobyl," Speech given to the 1987 annual meeting of the American Association for the Advancement of Science (AAAS), February 1987, in Chicago, Illinois.
39. Lindahl, AAAS speech.
40. Gale, AAAS speech.
41. IAEA, "The Puzzle of Chernobyl," *IEEE Spectrum Magazine* (July 1986), 40.
42. Ibid.
43. Ibid.
44. Leverett, AAAS speech.
45. Ibid.

CHAPTER 6
1. F. W. Gilbert, "Decontamination of the Canadian Reactor," *Chemical Engineering Progress* (May 1954), 268; Derula Murphy, *Nuclear Stakes* (New York: Ticknor & Fields, 1982), 76.
2. Ibid., 268.
3. "Perhaps the Worst, Not the First," *Time*, 12 May 1986, 50.
4. Alan Wyatt, *The Nuclear Challenge* (New York: The Book Press Limited, 1978), 77.
5. Hartley Howe, "World's First Atomic Alarm," *Popular Science* (October 1958), 238.
6. Ibid., 95.
7. Abbots and Nader, *The Menace of Atomic Energy*, 94.
8. Ibid.
9. Ibid., 218.
10. Ibid., 95.
11. Natalie Angler, "A Shipwreck Sends a Warning," *Time*, 10 September 1984, 33.
12. Tom Morganthau and Daniel Pederson, "Kerr-McGee's Deadly Cloud," *Newsweek*, 20 January 1986, 23.
13. David E. Kaplan, "When Incidents Are Accidents," *Oceans* (July 1983), 27.
14. Ibid., 30.
15. Ibid., 29.
16. "Mystery of the Scorpion: What Could Have Sunk It," *U.S. News & World Report*, 17 June 1968, 78.
17. Kaplan, "When Incidents Are Accidents," 31.

18. Ibid.
19. "Death on a Soviet Sub," *Newsweek*, 13 October 1953, 51.

CHAPTER 7
1. "Smog," *U.S., News & World Report* (December 1953), 77.
2. Gates, *Energy and Ecology*, 209.
3. Ibid., 336-39.
4. Ibid., 100.

CHAPTER 8
1. Peter Beckman, *The Health Hazards of NOT Going Nuclear* (New York: The Golem Press, 1976), 11-13.
2. Abbots and Nader, 365-67.
3. Bernard Cohen, *Before It's too Late: A Scientist's Case for Nuclear Energy* (New York: Plenum Press, 1983), 49-79.
4. Abbots and Nader, 109-113.
5. Cohen, *Before It's too Late*, 11-43.
6. Gofman and Tamplin, *Poisoned Power*, 149-70 and Abbots and Nader, 77-81.
7. "Too Hot for Burial," *Time*, 10 January 1983, 19.
8. Cohen, *Before It's too Late*, 234-35.
9. Abbots and Nader, 220.
10. Walter C. Patterson, *Nuclear Power* (New York: Penguin Books, 1986), 86.
11. Abbots and Nader, 224.

SOURCES

Abbots, John, and Ralph Nader. *The Menace of Atomic Energy.* New York: W. W. Norton & Co. 1977.

Adams, Herbert L. "How Radiation Victims Suffer." *Bulletin of Atomic Scientists* (August/September 1986).

Angler, Natalie. "A Shipwreck Sends a Warning." *Time* (10 September 1984), 33.

Barnathan, Joyce, and Steven Strasser. "Meltdown." *Newsweek* (12 May 1986), 20-30.

Beckman, Peter. *The Health Hazards of NOT Going Nuclear.* New York: The Golem Press, 1976.

"Breakdown Blessing." *Newsweek* (19 January 1953), 50.

Chase, William. "Chernobyl's Fiery Story Emerges." *U.S. News & World Report* (19 May 1986), 23.

"Chernobyl: New Estimates of Deaths, Concerns for the Food Chain." *Environment* (September 1986), 22.

"The Chernobyl Accident and Consequences." Public Affairs and Information Program, Atomic Industrial Forum, Inc. (July 1986).

Cohen, Bernard. *Before It's too Late: A Scientist's Case for Nuclear Energy.* New York: Plenum Press, 1983.

"Deadly Meltdown." *Time* (12 May 1986).

"Death on a Soviet Sub." *Newsweek* (13 October 1953).

Dickson, David, and Colin Norman. "The Aftermath of Chernobyl." *Science.* (5 September 1986), 1141-43.

Dollezhal, N. A. "Graphite-water Steam-generating Reactors in the U.S.S.R." *Nuclear Energy* (October 1981), 385-90.

"Emergency Planning." Public Affairs and Information Program, Atomic Industrial Forum, Inc. (July 1986).

Gabor, Andrea. "Thinking the Unthinkable: Can It Happen Here?" *U.S. News & World Report* (12 May 1986), 22-23.

Gale, Robert, M.D. "The Medical Consequences of Chernobyl." Speech given to the annual meeting of the American Association for the Advancement of Science (AAAS), February 1987, in Chicago, Illinois.

Gates, David M. *Energy and Ecology.* Sunderland, MA: Sinauer Publishers, Inc., 1985.

Gilbert, F. W. "Decontamination of the Canadian Reactor." *Chemical Engineering Progress* (May 1954), 267-271.

Gofman, John, and Arthur Tamplin. *Poisoned Power.* Emmaus, PA: Rodale Press, 1971.

Greenhalgh, Geoffrey. "Benefitting from Standardization in Russia and Eastern Europe." *Nuclear Engineering International.* Vol. 31 (August 1983), 26-29.

Greenwald, John. "More Fallout from Chernobyl." *Time* (19 May 1986), 44-66.

Herbert, W. "TMI Uncertainty Is Causing Chronic Stress." *Science News* (8 May 1982), 308.

Howe, Hartley. "World's First Atomic Alarm." *Popular Science* (October 1958), 92-95, 238-42.

International Atomic Energy Agency.

Josephson, Paul. "The Historical Roots of Chernobyl." Speech given to the 1987 annual meeting of the American Association for the Advancement of Science (AAAS), February 1987, in Chicago, Illinois.

Kaplan, David E. "When Incidents Are Accidents." *Oceans* (July 1983), 23-33.

Kurtis, Bill. "Reporting the News from Chernobyl." Speech given to the 1987 annual meeting of the American Association for the Advancement of Science (AAAS), February 1987, in Chicago, Illinois.

Leverett, Miles. "Chernobyl: Lessons for U.S. Science and Technology." Speech given to the 1987 annual meeting of the American Association for the Advancement of Science (AAAS), February 1987, in Chicago, Illinois.

Lindahl, Ingemar. "The Geopolitical Dimension," Speech delivered to the 1987 annual meeting of the American Association for the Advancement of Science (AAAS), February 1987, in Chicago, Illinois.

Marbach, William. "Cleaning Up the Mess." *Newsweek* (12 May 1986).

Martin, Daniel. *Three Mile Island.* Cambridge, MA: Ballinger Publishing Company, 1980.

Morganthau, Tom, and Daniel Pederson. "Kerr-McGee's Deadly Cloud." *Newsweek* (20 January 1986), 23.

Murphy, Derula. *Nuclear Stakes.* New York: Ticknor & Fields, 1982.

"Mystery of the Scorpion: What Could Have Sunk It." *U.S. News & World Report* (17 June 1968), 78.

Norman, Colin. "Chernobyl: Errors and Design Flaws." *Science* (5 September 1986), 1029-1031.

Patterson, Walter. "Breeder Reactor Politics in Europe," *Bulletin of the Atomic Scientist* (May 1986), 38-40.

_____. *Nuclear Power.* New York: Penguin Books, 1986.

Potter, Peter. "RBMK 1000—What the British Thought." *Nuclear Engineering International* (June 1986), 14.

"Protection of Environment." Code of Federal Regulations, Vol. 40 (1986).

Raloff, J. "Controversy Over Nuclear Evacuation Planning." *Science News* (14 February 1987), 100.

"RBMK 1000 Design." *Nuclear Engineering International* (June 1987), 7.

Reinhardt, William. "Meltdown Dooms Soviet Reactor." *Engineering News Record.* (8 May 1986), 10-12.

_____. "Soviet Reactor Was Flawed." *Engineering News Record* (30 May 1986), 16.

Rippon, Simon. "Chernobyl: The Soviet Report." *Nuclear News* (October 1986), 59-66.

Rogovin, Mitchell. *Three Mile Island: A Report to the Commissioners and to the Public.* Nuclear Regulatory Commission Special Inquiry Group, (1980).

Semenov, B. A. "Nuclear Power in the Soviet Union." *IAEA Bulletin.* Vol. 25, No. 2, 47-59.

"Smog." *U. S. News & World Report* (18 December 1953), 77.

Stephens, Mark. *Three Mile Island, The Hour-by-Hour Account of What Really Happened.* New York: Random House, 1980.

"TMI-1 Restart Underway." *Science News* (12 October 1985), 229.

"TMI—Technical Blow by Blow." IEEE *Spectrum Magazine* (November 1979).

"Too Hot for the Usual Burial." *Time* (10 January 1983), 19.

Trafford, Abigail, and Stanley Wellborn. "Stark Fallout." *U.S. News & World Report* (12 May 1986), 18-21.

"2 Reactors Are Canceled." *The New York Times* (26 April 1987), Sec. 1, 16.

Wyatt, Alan. *The Nuclear Challenge.* New York: The Book Press Limited, 1978.

SUGGESTED READINGS

Asimov, Isaac. *How Did We Find Out about Nuclear Power?* New York: Walker and Company, 1976.

Bronowski, J. *The Ascent of Man;* Chapters 10 & 11. Boston: Little, Brown and Company, 1973.

Cohen, Bernard. *Before It's too Late: A Scientist's Case for Nuclear Energy.* New York: Plenum Press, 1983.

Gallant, Roy A. *Explorers of the Atom.* Garden City, New York: Doubleday and Company, 1974.

Goode, Stephen. *The Nuclear Energy Controversy.* New York: Franklin Watts, 1980.

Kaku, Michio, and Jennifer Trainer, editors. *Nuclear Power: Both Sides.* New York: W. W. Norton & Company, 1982.

Lampton, Christopher. *Fusion, the Eternal Flame.* New York: Franklin Watts, 1982.

McPhee, John. *The Curve of Binding Energy.* New York: Farrar, Straus, and Giroux, 1973.

Nader, Ralph, and John Abbot. *The Menace of Atomic Energy.* New York: W.W. Norton & Co., 1977.

Stepp, Ann. *The Story of Radioactivity.* Irvington-on-Hudson, New York: Harvey House, 1971.

INDEX